For Pasta Lovers

For Pasta Lovers

Joseph Vitale

KEY PORTER BOOKS

Canadian Cataloguing in Publication Data

Vitale, Joseph, 1938–
    For pasta lovers

Includes index.
ISBN 1-55263-287-3

1. Cookery (Pasta). I. Title.

TX809.M17V57 2000   641.8'22   C00-931685-X

The Canada Council | Le Conseil des Arts
For the Arts | du Canada
since 1957 | depuis 1957

The publisher gratefully acknowledges the support of the Canada Council for the Arts and the Ontario Arts Council for its publishing program.

We acknowledge the financial support of the Government of Canada through the Book Publishing Industry Development Program (BPIDP) for our publishing activities.

Key Porter Books Limited
70 The Esplanade
Toronto, Ontario
Canada M5E 1R2

www.keyporter.com

Electronic formatting: Heidy Lawrance Associates

Printed and bound in Italy

01 02 03 04   6 5 4 3 2

Table of Contents

Letter from the President

At ITALPASTA, we believe that good people working toward a common goal can accomplish anything they set out to do. As the founder and owner of ITALPASTA, it has been one of my own longtime goals to produce a cookbook that would serve the needs of our loyal customers.

It is, after all, loyal customers that have made the company such a success. ITALPASTA opened its doors back in 1989, on 55,000 square feet of property in Brampton, Ontario. Along with about 10 full-time employees, I set out to realize another one of my goals. After years of experience in Canada's pasta industry, I had come to realize that there were essentially two dominant manufacturers, both of which were owned and operated out of the United States. There was a definite need for a Canadian-run manufacturer.

After more than 10 years in business, ITALPASTA is now a major force in the industry. We sell coast-to-coast in Canada, and distribute our products in the United States, the Caribbean, the Philippines, Asia, and Israel. Our staff has grown to more than 230, and our office space and warehouse now take up 250,000 square feet, still in Brampton. All of this was made possible by the men and women who have supported ITALPASTA and its products over the years.

It's time to give something back. *For Pasta Lovers* is our way of saying "thank you" for the support and patronage we've received over the years. This exquisite cookbook showcases unique and delicious pasta dishes that meet the high standards of authentic Italian cuisine. It also provides useful information about pasta, and how to make the most of this wonderful staple.

Now that I have achieved *my* goals, we at ITALPASTA would like to help others realize theirs. With our corporate belief in tradition, and the value of family and loved ones, it is with pleasure that we donate all profits from *For Pasta Lovers* to Big Brothers and Big Sisters organizations across Canada. The Big Brothers and Big Sisters movement reaches out to children needing friends, and pairs them with caring adult volunteers. The immense support that these mentor friendships produce can truly change a child's quality of life and hopes for the future.

Enjoy *For Pasta Lovers*. In purchasing it, you have done something good for yourself — and for the children in your community who need your help.

Sincerely,

Joseph Vitale
President
ITALPASTA LIMITED

Joseph Vitale and his mother, Nicoletta.

Introduction

Growing up in Italy, you become accustomed to fine food. It's everywhere you go — from the fresh air markets of the smallest towns to the kitchens of Rome's restaurants and cafés. If you're lucky, it's also on your own table.

It was certainly on mine. As a child in Modugno, Bari — a small town in southwestern Italy's Puglia region — I came to expect a certain level of quality in my food. My grandfather traded in the region's famous olive oil, nuts, and semolina, and my mother used these ingredients in her kitchen. Memories of the delicious results have stayed with me throughout the years. Even when I was away at the seminary school, I did whatever I could to ensure a good meal.

Nearly 50 years later, I'm still committed to putting fine food on the table — my own table and yours. That's what this cookbook is all about. Over the years, I've learned a lot about making pasta, in all of its various forms. After more than 30 years in the business, I can tell you anything you want to know about wheat, nutritional content, and the numerous products that we eat alongside, or on top, of our pasta. But that's not what makes *For Pasta Lovers* so special.

What I'd really like to share with you, in the pages that follow, is the knowledge I've brought with me from Italy — the knowledge passed down from my grandfather and my mother. I'll tell you how to choose the best vegetables and cheeses. I'll offer hints on serving and presenting your pasta creations. You'll learn about how certain flavors blend to create unforgettable taste sensations. I'll share my favorite recipes, with the hope that they'll become your favorites as well.

Years ago, back home in Italy, I overheard a shopkeeper tell my mother that her tomato sauce would only be as good as the ingredients she put into it. I've always remembered that, and I've committed myself to providing my customers with the quality foods they need to serve the very best. When you cook — whether it's with spaghetti, gnocchi, olive oil, or canned tomatoes — use the best ingredients you can afford. Your tastebuds, and your guests, will thank you.

Enjoy *For Pasta Lovers* — and may all of your meals be memorable.

How to Cook Pasta

Pasta, whether made fresh or dried, should be cooked with care in a large saucepan in plenty of boiling water (about 3 L/12 cups for each 1 lb/500 g of pasta). Salt should be added to the water just before the pasta. Do not add oil to the cooking water. Although adding oil will prevent the pasta from sticking together, it will also prevent the sauce from adhering to the pasta! (However, ITALPASTA is made of high grade durum semolina and therefore will not stick together.)

When cooking pastas:

✧ Bring a large pot of water to a boil.

✧ Add salt. The recipes in this book call for 1-2 tbsp (15-25 mL) of salt.

✧ Add pasta and stir to ensure that it does not stick. Return to a boil and cook, stirring occasionally, until the pasta is *al dente* (tender but still firm to the bite). Do not overcook pasta. Remember that it will continue to cook slightly even after it has been drained.

✧ Drain the pasta and transfer to a warm serving dish or to the skillet with the sauce, depending on the instructions in the recipe. Do not overdrain pasta or it will become dry and absorb too much sauce.

✧ Do not let pasta sit while waiting for the sauce to be done.

✧ Toss the pasta with the sauce until it is well coated — do not oversauce. Serve at once!

✧ If the pasta is to be baked, undercook it slightly or it will become too soft after baking.

CHAPTER ONE

Pasta with Seafood

In Italy, you are never far from the Mediterranean and its rich variety of seafood: eels from Comacchio, soft shell crabs from Trieste, mullet caught off the Tremiti Islands, lobster from Sardinia, mussels from Taranto, tuna from the Gulf of Naples. For centuries, this bounty has been an important part of the country's diet and Italian cooks have been wonderfully inventive in combining seafood with pasta.

Farfalle con Salmone

(PASTA BOW TIES WITH SALMON)

Of all fish, salmon ranks among my favorites. Quick to cook, a melt-in-your-mouth texture, and as good with just a squeeze of lemon as it is with the many sauces that complement it. A fabulous tribute to a small pasta like farfalle.

Makes 4 servings

2 tbsp	butter	25 mL
1	small onion, finely diced	1
3	cloves garlic, finely chopped	3
2 cups	mushrooms, sliced	500 mL
1½ lb	fillet of salmon, diced into ½-inch (1 cm) pieces	750 g
2 tbsp	fresh basil, chopped	25 mL
1 tsp	rosemary	5 mL
1 tsp	oregano	5 mL
3 tbsp	brandy	45 mL
¼ cup	dry white wine	50 mL
1 cup	tomato sauce (page 121)	250 mL
¼ tsp	salt	1 mL
¼ tsp	black pepper, freshly ground	1 mL
1 lb	ITALPASTA Small Bow Ties	500 g

1. Bring a large pot of lightly salted water to a boil.
2. Meanwhile, in a large skillet, sauté the onion and garlic in the butter over medium heat until the onion is clear. Add the mushrooms and continue to sauté until they begin to soften.
3. Add the salmon, basil, rosemary, and oregano and sauté for another 1 to 2 minutes, or until the salmon is half cooked.
4. Add the brandy and wine, and reduce by simmering for another minute or two.
5. Add the tomato sauce, season with salt and pepper, and simmer until the salmon is cooked through. Do not let the sauce boil rapidly. This will cause the salmon to break apart. Remove from the heat when the salmon is cooked, about 2 minutes.
6. When the water is boiling, cook the pasta *al dente*. Drain well and add the pasta to the salmon. Toss or stir thoroughly, but gently. Place on a warm serving dish or individual plates and serve immediately.

Farfalle con Pesce Spade e Erbe

(PASTA BOW TIES WITH SWORDFISH AND TARRAGON)

Swordfish is a wonderfully firm and flavorful fish that can have the texture of chicken and — like all fish and seafood — requires very little time to cook. A good replacement for swordfish (it can be very expensive) is shark. It has the same meaty consistency and similar flavor.

Makes 4 to 6 servings

2 tbsp	ITALPASTA olive oil	25 mL
2 tbsp	butter, divided	25 mL
4	shallots, finely chopped	4
4	cloves of garlic, finely chopped	4
2 cups	mushrooms, sliced	500 mL
1½ lb	swordfish, cut into 1-inch (2.5 cm) cubes	750 g
pinch	black pepper, freshly ground	pinch
pinch	salt	pinch
3 tbsp	fresh tarragon, coarsely chopped	45 mL
1	sweet red pepper, diced	1
1	green pepper, diced	1
2	lemons, zest only, coarsely chopped	2
	additional pepper	
½ cup	dry white wine	125 mL
2 tbsp	lemon juice	25 mL
½ cup	chicken stock (page 123)	125 mL
1 lb	ITALPASTA Large Bow Ties	500 g
1 cup	Parmesan cheese, freshly grated	250 mL
1	lemon, cut into wedges for garnish	1
	parsley, for garnish	

1. Using a large saucepan or skillet, heat the oil and 1 tbsp (15 mL) of the butter over medium heat. Add the shallots and garlic and slowly sauté until they begin to soften. Do not let them brown. Add the mushrooms and continue to cook until they begin to soften.
2. Season the swordfish cubes with salt and pepper. Increase the heat slightly and add the fish to the pan. Add the tarragon and continue to sauté until the fish begins to brown. At this point, the swordfish should be about half cooked. Add the remaining butter, red and green peppers, lemon zest, additional black pepper, and white wine. The heat of the pan should immediately reduce the wine. Add the lemon juice and chicken stock and simmer until most of the liquid has been boiled away, about 3 to 5 minutes. Remove from heat.
3. Bring a large pot of lightly salted water to a boil, cook the pasta *al dente*, and drain. Put the saucepan back on the stove on medium-high heat. Add the pasta to the swordfish and sprinkle with the Parmesan cheese. Mix or toss gently and serve at once, garnished with additional Parmesan cheese, parsley, and lemon wedges.

Fettuccine con Calamari e Aglio

(FETTUCCINE WITH SQUID AND GARLIC)

imple and quick dish that will refresh your senses. But you do have to be a garlic lover.

kes 4 servings

2 tbsp	butter	25 mL
2 tbsp	ITALPASTA olive oil	25 mL
6	cloves garlic, finely chopped	6
6	shallots, diced	6
2 lb	squid, cleaned and cut into ¼-inch (5 mm) rings, tentacles left whole	1 kg
pinch	salt	pinch
pinch	pepper	pinch
½ lb	ITALPASTA Fettuccine	250 g
pinch	chili pepper flakes	pinch
1 cup	dry white wine	250 mL
	juice of 1 lemon	
½ cup	Parmesan cheese, freshly grated	125 mL
pinch	chopped parsley	pinch
	additional Parmesan cheese, freshly grated	

Bring a large pot of lightly salted water to a boil.
Meanwhile, heat the butter and oil in a large skillet. Add the garlic and shallots and sauté briefly. Do not burn. Add the squid, salt, and pepper. Turn the heat to medium and sauté, tossing and moving the ingredients frequently. Add the chili pepper flakes to the seafood, and when the squid is almost cooked (the rings will be opaque, and tentacles pink), add the wine and lemon juice. Simmer until the liquid is reduced by half. Remove from heat. When the water is boiling, cook the pasta *al dente*, then drain well. Add the pasta, Parmesan cheese and parsley to the squid mixture. Toss or stir well and serve with additional Parmesan cheese, if desired.

Fettuccine con Frutti di Mare e Salsa di Pomodoro

(FETTUCCINE WITH SEAFOOD IN A SPICY TOMATO SAUCE)

A seafood extravaganza. Make sure that you have enough Italian crusty bread to clean the plates after the pasta and seafood are devoured.

Makes 4 to 6 servings

2 tbsp	butter	25 mL
1 tbsp	ITALPASTA olive oil	15 mL
3	large cloves garlic, finely minced	3
1	onion, diced	1
2	stalks celery, diced	2
1	28-oz (796 mL) tin ITALPASTA Italian plum tomatoes (seedless and diced) with juice	1
1 cup	dry red wine	250 mL
5	fresh basil leaves, chopped	5
1 tsp	chili pepper flakes (or to taste)	5 mL
pinch	salt	pinch
pinch	white pepper	pinch
16	large mussels, scrubbed and beards removed	16
16	clams, cleaned and scrubbed	16
½ lb	large shrimp, peel on and deveined	250 g
½ lb	scallops, cut in half if large	250 g
1 lb	ITALPASTA Fettuccine	500 g
5	sprigs fresh parsley, finely chopped	5
	Parmesan cheese, freshly grated	

1. Bring a large pot of lightly salted water to a boil.
2. In a large skillet or pot, heat the butter and oil and sauté the garlic, onion, and celery until golden brown. Add the tomatoes, red wine, basil, chili pepper flakes, salt, and white pepper and simmer until mixture is reduced by a third. Taste for seasoning, stirring constantly.
3. When the sauce is slightly thickened and full of flavor, add the mussels and clams. Cover and simmer until the shells have opened, about 3 to 5 minutes. Discard any clams or mussels that remain closed.
4. Add the shrimp and scallops and continue to simmer until they are firm and the shrimp have turned red (2 or 3 minutes), stirring constantly.
5. When the water is boiling, cook the pasta *al dente* and drain well. Add the cooked pasta to the sauce, toss or stir well, and simmer until the pasta is hot. Transfer to a serving dish and garnish with parsley and Parmesan cheese.

ttuccine con Calamari e Aglio

Fusilli Lunghi con Gamberi e Finocchio
(FUSILLI PASTA WITH SHRIMP AND FRESH FENNEL)

Fennel is an aromatic flowering plant of Italian origin that has a slight flavor of licorice (aniseed). It is cooked somewhat like celery and is widely used to flavor a great many dishes. Try this one with fusilli and shrimp.

Makes 4 to 6 servings

¼ cup	ITALPASTA extra virgin olive oil	50 mL
5	cloves garlic, finely chopped	5
3 cups	fresh fennel, tops removed, and bulbs sliced very thinly lengthwise	750 mL
¼ cup	water	50 mL
5	fresh plum tomatoes, peeled, seeded, and diced into ¼-inch (5mm) pieces	5
1½ lb	medium shrimp, peeled, deveined, and cut in half	750 g
2 tsp	fresh marjoram, chopped (or 1 tsp/5 mL dried)	10 mL
¼ tsp	salt	1 mL
pinch	black pepper, freshly ground	pinch
1 lb	ITALPASTA Fusilli	500 g

1. Bring a pot of lightly salted water to a boil.
2. Meanwhile, heat the oil in a large skillet and, over medium heat, sauté the garlic until it is sizzling but not browned. Stir in the fennel so that it is well coated with oil. Add a quarter cup (50 mL) of water, turn the heat down, and cook semi-covered for about 5 minutes or until the fennel is tender.
3. Remove the lid and stir in the diced tomatoes. Simmer until any extra liquid has evaporated.
4. Add the shrimp and marjoram to the sauce and season with salt and pepper. Simmer for about 2 minutes or until the shrimp is cooked. Remove from the heat and set aside while you prepare the pasta.
5. When the water is boiling, cook the pasta *al dente*. Drain well, then return the seafood to the stove and add the pasta. Toss or stir well and serve immediately.

Fusilli con Salmone e Panna
(FUSILLI WITH SALMON IN A CREAMY TOMATO SAUCE)

A gentle blend of plum tomatoes and cream help to create this delicate salmon and pasta entrée.

Makes 4 to 6 servings

1½ lb	salmon fillets, skinless and cut into 1-inch (2.5 cm) strips	750 g
¼ tsp	salt	1 mL
¼ tsp	white pepper	1 mL
¼ cup	flour	50 mL
2 tbsp	butter, divided	25 mL
2 tbsp	ITALPASTA olive oil, divided	25 mL
2	cloves garlic, finely chopped	2
5	green onions, diced	5
½ lb	mushrooms, quartered	250 g
3 tbsp	capers	45 mL
8	fresh plum tomatoes, peeled, seeded, and diced	8
½ cup	dry white wine	125 mL
¼ cup	whipping cream	50 mL
2 tbsp	Parmesan cheese	25 mL
1 lb	ITALPASTA Fusilli	500 g
5	sprigs parsley, chopped	5

1. Bring a pot of lightly salted water to a boil.
2. Meanwhile, season the salmon strips with a little salt and pepper and dust with flour, shaking off the excess. Heat half of the butter and oil in a large skillet and sauté the salmon until brown. Remove from the pan with a slotted spoon and set aside. Discard the oil in the pan.
3. Add the remaining butter and oil to the skillet. Sauté garlic, onions, mushrooms, and capers until the mushrooms are soft. Add the tomatoes, with salt, and pepper, and simmer until the sauce is reduced by a third.
4. Add the whipping cream and Parmesan cheese, and simmer until slightly thickened.
5. While the sauce is thickening, cook the pasta *al dente*.
6. Just before the pasta is done, gently add the salmon to the sauce and continue simmering until the salmon is cooked, about 1 to 2 minutes. Drain the pasta, place on a serving dish, and cover gently with the sauce so as not to break the salmon. Sprinkle with parsley and serve immediately.

Fettuccine di Spinaci con Cozze e Panna

(SPINACH FETTUCCINE WITH MUSSELS ALFREDO)

the countless varieties of pasta and sauces, Fettuccine Alfredo would have to be my all-time favorite. is recipe adds a little twist. I don't know if Chef Alfredo would condone this recipe, but I'll let you be e judge.

akes 2 servings

1 cup	dry white wine	250 mL
1 cup	water	250 mL
1	onion, diced	1
1½ lb	mussels, scrubbed and beards removed	750 g
1 tbsp	butter	15 mL
1½ cups	whipping cream	375 mL
pinch	salt	pinch
pinch	white pepper	pinch
¼ tsp	nutmeg	1 mL
¼ cup	Parmesan cheese	50 mL
½ lb	ITALPASTA Spinach Fettuccine	250 g
2	sprigs parsley, finely chopped	2

Mix the wine, water, and onion in a large skillet. Bring to a boil and add the mussels. Steam, covered, until the mussels have opened, discarding any that remain closed. Remove the mussels and strain the liquid, keeping both reserved separately.

In the same skillet, add the butter, cream, and 2 tbsp (25 mL) of the reserved liquid. Season with salt, pepper, and nutmeg. Bring to a boil and then let simmer. Whisk in the Parmesan cheese and continue to simmer until mixture has thickened slightly. Remove from heat.

Meanwhile, bring a large pot of lightly salted water to a boil. Cook the pasta *al dente* and drain well.

Add the cooked mussels (with shells) to the cream sauce and bring back to a boil.

Add the pasta to the cream sauce and toss or stir well. Serve immediately on a large platter or individual plates, sprinkled with Parmesan cheese and parsley.

Vermicelli con Conchiglie e Pomodori

(VERMICELLI WITH SCALLOPS AND TOMATO)

Scallops, when cooked properly, have a marvelous texture and melt in your mouth like no other food. Overcook these morsels though, and their magic is gone. Here is one of my many scallop recipes. Let its magic work for you.

Makes 4 to 6 servings

1 lb	ITALPASTA Vermicelli	500 g
2 tbsp	butter	25 mL
1 tbsp	ITALPASTA olive oil	15 mL
3	shallots, finely chopped	3
3	cloves garlic, finely chopped	3
1½	scallops, cut in half if large	1½
4	plum tomatoes, peeled, seeded, and diced	4
1 cup	whipping cream	250 mL
¼ cup	dry white wine	50 mL
2 tsp	ITALPASTA tomato paste	10 mL
pinch	salt	pinch
pinch	pepper	pinch
pinch	nutmeg	pinch
2 tbsp	fresh parsley, chopped	25 mL

1. Cook the pasta in lightly salted boiling water *al dente*. Drain well and set aside.
2. Heat the butter and oil in a large frying pan and sauté the shallots and garlic until soft, about 2 minutes. Add the scallops and continue to sauté until lightly browned or about half cooked. Remove scallops from the pan.
3. Add the diced tomatoes, cream, wine, tomato paste, salt, pepper, and nutmeg and simmer for about 5 minutes or until the sauce begins to thicken. Return the scallops to the pan and simmer for another 1 to 2 minutes or until the scallops are cooked.
4. Add the pasta to the sauce and toss so that the pasta is well-coated and hot. With a large fork, put the pasta onto a large serving dish or individual plates and spoon the sauce over top. Sprinkle with parsley and serve at once.

Capellini al Salmone con Asparagi e Erbe
(CAPELLINI WITH SALMON, ASPARAGUS AND DILL)

There is a wonderful three-way marriage between salmon, asparagus, and dill. Served hot or at room temperature, tossed with steaming hot pasta as an entrée or an appetizer, this is a dish that I always come back to and I know that you will, too.

Makes 4 to 6 servings

12	thick spears of asparagus, cleaned, trimmed, and cut into 1-inch (2.5 cm) pieces	12
2 tbsp	butter	25 mL
1 tbsp	ITALPASTA olive oil	15 mL
1½ lb	fresh salmon fillets, cut into ½-inch (1 cm) wide strips	750 g
5 (or ½ cup)	scallions, coarsely chopped	5 (or 125 mL)
4 tbsp	fresh dill, coarsely chopped	50 mL
2 tbsp	fresh parsley, coarsely chopped	25 mL
2 tsp	capers	10 mL
1 cup	dry white wine	250 mL
2 tbsp	lemon juice	25 mL
1 lb	ITALPASTA Capellini	500 g
¼ cup	Parmesan cheese, freshly grated	50 mL
¼ cup	Romano cheese, freshly grated	50 mL
	additional parsley, dill, and Parmesan for final sprinkling and garnish	
¼ tsp	black pepper, freshly ground	1 mL

1. Bring a large pot of lightly salted water to a boil for the pasta.
2. Bring a smaller pot of water to a boil and cook the asparagus so that it is still crunchy. Rinse in cold water, drain, and set aside for later use.
3. Heat the butter and oil in a large skillet and brown the salmon pieces on both sides. While you are cooking the second side of the fish, add the scallions, dill, cooked asparagus, parsley, and capers to the pan. Stir in gently so as not to break the salmon pieces. Add the white wine and lemon juice and let simmer until the liquid has almost completely evaporated or until the salmon is cooked and tender, about 2 minutes.
4. Meanwhile, cook the pasta *al dente*. Drain and add to the salmon.
5. Add the Parmesan and Romano cheeses, toss or stir gently, and serve garnished with additional parsley, dill, cheese, and freshly ground black pepper.

Capellini con Conchiglia e Zafferano
(CAPELLINI WITH A CREAMY SCALLOP AND SAFFRON SAUCE)

The delicate flavor of the scallops, cream, and brandy combined with this delicate pasta makes this dish one of my favorites.

Makes 2 to 4 servings

2 tbsp	butter	25 mL
3	shallots (or 1 small onion, diced)	3
1	large clove garlic, finely chopped	1
2 cups	mushrooms, sliced	500 mL
¼ cup	flour	50 mL
1 lb	sea scallops	500 g
1	medium sweet red pepper, diced	1
1¼ oz	brandy	40 mL
¼ cup	dry white wine	50 mL
1 cup	whipping cream	250 mL
¼ tsp	salt	1 mL
¼ tsp	white pepper	1 mL
1 tsp	dried saffron	5 mL
½ lb	ITALPASTA Capellini	250 g
2 tbsp	parsley, chopped	25 mL

1. Bring a large pot of lightly salted water to a boil.
2. Heat the butter in a large skillet or frying pan. Add the shallots and garlic and sauté until sizzling, but not brown. Add the mushrooms and continue to sauté for about a minute until they have softened.
3. Dust the scallops in the flour and shake off any excess. Add the scallops to the pan and continue to sauté over medium-high heat for no more than 1½ minutes. The scallops will be about a quarter cooked.
4. Add the red pepper, toss or stir, then add the brandy and flambé if you like (not necessary), then add the white wine and cream. Season with salt, pepper and saffron. Continue to cook until the sauce begins to thicken. If the sauce has not thickened and the scallops are cooked and tender, remove them with a slotted spoon. When the sauce has thickened slightly, replace the scallops and remove the pan from the heat.
5. When the water boils, cook the pasta *al dente*. Drain and add the pasta to the sauce. Add the parsley and toss or stir well. Place the pasta on a serving dish or individual plates and pour the sauce over the pasta. Garnish with parsley, and serve immediately.

Linguine con Frutti di Mare e Panna
(LINGUINE WITH SHRIMP AND SCALLOPS IN A CREAM SAUCE)

Cream and Dijon mustard are ingredients commonly used in the northern regions of Italy where the cuisine is heavily influenced by the Swiss and the French. You will find that nutmeg is a nice addition to most any recipe that calls for cream.

Makes 2 to 4 servings

2 tbsp	butter	25 mL
1 tbsp	ITALPASTA olive oil	15 mL
1	small onion, diced	1
2 cups	mushrooms, sliced	500 mL
¼ lb	shrimp, peeled and deveined	125 g
¼ lb	sea scallops	125 g
1 cup	whipping cream	250 mL
¼ cup	brandy	50 mL
¼ cup	dry white wine	50 mL
1 tbsp	Dijon mustard	15 mL
pinch	salt	pinch
pinch	white pepper	pinch
pinch	nutmeg	pinch
½ lb	ITALPASTA Linguine	250 g
2 tbsp	Parmesan cheese, freshly grated	25 mL
2 tbsp	fresh parsley, chopped	25 mL

Heat the butter and oil in a large frying pan. Add the onions and mushrooms and sauté until soft.

Add the shrimp and scallops to the pan and sauté over medium to high heat until partially cooked, about 1 minute. Add the cream, brandy, wine, and Dijon. Stir well to blend the mustard. Season with salt, pepper, and nutmeg. Simmer until the seafood is cooked and the sauce is slightly reduced, about 2 minutes.

Meanwhile, bring a large pot of lightly salted water to a boil and cook the linguine *al dente*. Drain, then add the pasta to the seafood mixture. Toss or stir well. Place on a serving dish and sprinkle with Parmesan cheese and parsley. Serve immediately.

Linguine alle Vongole
(LINGUINE WITH CLAMS)

There is a love affair between clam sauce and garlic. I believe that you can never use too much garlic in this dish. A staple in most Italian restaurants, this dish has many variations. The common factor is that the pasta needs to soak in the wonderful flavors of the sauce. Also ranked as one of my favorites.

Makes 2 to 4 servings

2 tbsp	butter	25 mL
4	cloves garlic, finely chopped	4
4	green onions, diced	4
1	5-oz (150 g) tin baby clams, with juice	1
24	whole clams (small size), cleaned and scrubbed	
1 cup	dry white wine	250 mL
1 lb	ITALPASTA Linguine	500 g
	Parmesan cheese, freshly grated	
3	sprigs parsley, finely chopped	3

1. Bring a large pot of lightly salted water to a boil.
2. Meanwhile, heat butter in a large skillet and add the garlic and green onions. Sauté until tender. Add the baby clams (with juice) and the wine. Bring to a boil and add whole clams. Cover and simmer until clams have fully opened, about 5 minutes. Discard any that have not opened. Remove the meat from three-quarters of the clams, keeping the rest in the shell for garnish. Return all of the clams to the sauce and continue to simmer.
3. When the water has come to a boil, cook the pasta *al dente*. Drain and add the pasta to the clam sauce. Toss or stir to mix well, and simmer for 3 to 5 minutes to let the pasta absorb the sauce and its flavor.
4. Serve at once with Parmesan cheese and parsley as garnishes.

Linguine con Gamberetti "al Diavolo"
(LINGUINE WITH SHRIMP IN A SPICY TOMATO SAUCE)

A terrific dish to serve as an appetizer — it wakes up the taste buds and prepares them for the feast to come.

Makes 2 to 4 servings

1 tbsp	ITALPASTA olive oil	15 mL
2 tbsp	butter	25 mL
3	shallots, finely chopped	3
3	cloves garlic, minced	3
1½ lb	large shrimp, peeled and deveined	750 g
3 tbsp	brandy	45 mL
½ cup	red wine	125 mL
6	small plum tomatoes, peeled, seeded, and diced (or 3 large plum tomatoes)	6
1 tsp	ITALPASTA tomato paste	5 mL
2 tbsp	fresh basil, finely chopped	25 mL
½ tsp	oregano	2 mL
½ tsp	thyme	2 mL
¼ tsp	crushed chili peppers (more if desired)	1 mL
pinch	cayenne	pinch
pinch	salt	pinch
pinch	pepper	pinch
½ lb	ITALPASTA Linguine	250 g
	fresh basil leaves for garnish	

1. Bring a pot of lightly salted water to a boil.
2. Sauté the shallots and garlic in the oil and butter until soft. Add the shrimp and toss or stir well. Add the brandy, red wine, tomatoes, tomato paste, basil, oregano, thyme, chili pepper, and cayenne and stir well.
3. Cook over medium heat until the shrimp is done, about 2 to 3 minutes. If the shrimp is cooked and the sauce is too runny, remove the shrimp with a slotted spoon and continue to cook the sauce until it has reduced and thickened slightly. Add salt and pepper if desired.
4. In the meantime, cook the linguine *al dente* and drain.
5. Return the shrimp to the sauce and cook for a few seconds until the shrimp is hot. Add the cooked pasta to the sauce. Toss or stir well so that the pasta is coated with sauce.
6. With a large fork, put the pasta on a platter or in individual serving dishes and spoon the sauce and shrimp on top. Garnish with basil and serve immediately.

Linguine con Gamberetti e Funghi
(LINGUINE WITH SHRIMP AND WILD MUSHROOMS)

Although ginger and garlic give a hint of the Orient to a dish, I love the flavors created by the combination of these two ingredients. Along with my favorite seafood, they make this dish is a must-try!

Makes 2 to 4 servings

2 tbsp	butter	25 mL
4	shallots, finely diced	4
2 tsp	ginger root, finely diced	10 mL
4	cloves garlic, finely chopped	4
2	large portobello mushrooms, sliced	2
2 cups	oyster mushrooms, sliced	500 mL
¾ lb	large shrimp, shell on and deveined	375 g
½ cup	dry white wine	125 mL
½ cup	chicken stock (page 123)	125 mL
1 tbsp	Dijon mustard	15 mL
½ lb	ITALPASTA Linguine	250 g
4	sprigs parsley, finely chopped	4

1. Bring a large pot of lightly salted water to a boil.
2. Heat the butter in a large frying pan, add the shallots, ginger, and garlic and sauté until soft. Add the mushrooms and continue to sauté over medium to high heat until the mushrooms have softened, about 2 minutes.
3. Add the shrimp to the pan and sauté until they begin to turn red. Add the white wine, chicken stock, and Dijon mustard. Stir until the Dijon is fully mixed into the sauce. Continue to cook until the shrimp is done and the sauce is slightly reduced, about 2 minutes.
4. Add the pasta to the boiling water and cook *al dente*. Drain, then add the pasta and the parsley to the shrimp, toss or stir, and serve immediately, garnished with additional parsley.

Vermicelli con Frutti di Mare e Pesto

(VERMICELLI WITH SEAFOOD AND PESTO)

As I hope you have discovered by now, I am a great lover of seafood. I am also a great lover of pesto. This is a recipe I created for a symphony of my favorite flavors.

Makes 4 to 6 servings

1 lb	ITALPASTA Vermicelli	500 g
1	medium onion, diced	1
5	cloves garlic, chopped	5
2 tbsp	butter	25 mL
1 tbsp	ITALPASTA olive oil	15 mL
12	scallops	12
12	shrimps, peeled and deveined	12
12	mussels, scrubbed and beards removed	12
12	medium clams	12
5	squids, sliced into rings	5
2 tbsp	brandy	25 mL
¼ cup	dry white wine	50 mL
6	plum tomatoes, seeded and diced	6
¼ cup	pesto (page 121)	50 mL
¼ tsp	dried, crushed chili pepper	1 mL
1 tsp	sugar	5 mL
2 tbsp	fresh parsley, chopped	25 mL

1. Cook the pasta *al dente* in lightly salted boiling water, drain, and set aside.
2. Sauté the onion and garlic in the butter and olive oil until tender. Add the scallops, shrimp, squid, and the mussels and clams in their shells. Continue to cook about 2 minutes, stirring frequently.
3. Add the brandy, wine, tomatoes, pesto, chili peppers, and sugar. Simmer for about 2 minutes or until the seafood is cooked.
4. Stir in the drained pasta and coat with the sauce. Simmer for about 1 minute or until the pasta is hot.
5. Remove the mussels and clams (discard any that have not opened.) Place the pasta and sauce on a serving dish and arrange the mussels and clams around the pasta. Sprinkle with parsley and serve immediately.

Vermicelli con Gamberoni e Pernod

(VERMICELLI WITH PRAWNS AND ANISE)

My love for prawns is equaled only by my love of cooking these morsels. In this recipe, the Pernod or Anise (a licorice-flavored liqueur) is the predominate flavor of the sauce. By itself, it can be strong, but mixed with a little brandy or cognac, it's a true gourmet delight.

Makes 2 servings

½ lb	ITALPASTA Vermicelli	250 g
2 tbsp	butter	25 mL
3	shallots, finely diced	3
1 cup	mushrooms, finely chopped	250 mL
1 lb	fresh prawns, peeled and deveined	500 g
¼ cup	Pernod or Anise	50 mL
2 tbsp	brandy	25 mL
½ cup	whipping cream	125 mL
¼ cup	Parmesan cheese, freshly grated	50 mL
pinch	salt	pinch
pinch	pepper	pinch
pinch	nutmeg	pinch
dash	lemon juice	dash
	additional Parmesan cheese	
2 tbsp	fresh parsley, chopped	25 mL

1. Cook the pasta *al dente*, drain, and set aside.
2. Have a large pot of water simmering and ready to finish the pasta.
3. In a large skillet, melt the butter and sauté the shallots and mushrooms until soft but not browned. Add the prawns and continue to sauté over medium heat for 2 to 3 minutes. Add the Pernod and the brandy. Flambé if you like, then add the cream and Parmesan cheese. Season with salt, pepper, and nutmeg. Add the lemon juice and blend all ingredients well. When the sauce begins to bubble, it is done.
4. Put the cooked pasta in a large strainer and immerse in the simmering water for about 10 seconds. Shake off excess water and add pasta to the sauce. Toss or stir well and serve immediately. Sprinkle with Parmesan cheese and parsley.

Rotèlle con Calamari al Modo di Tapas
(WAGON WHEEL PASTA WITH SQUID, SPANISH STYLE)

This is a dish that I discovered in a Spanish Tapas bar. Add some pasta and Romano cheese and this makes a wonderful appetizer with bruschetta, garlic bread, or any crusty Italian bread.

Makes 4 servings

¼ cup	ITALPASTA olive oil	50 mL
1 cup	onion, finely chopped	250 mL
4	cloves garlic, finely chopped	4
½ cup	green Spanish olives, pitted and chopped	125 mL
½ tsp	saffron stems	2 mL
1 tbsp	ITALPASTA tomato paste	15 mL
1 cup	dry white wine	250 mL
1 cup	fish stock (page 123)	250 mL
1½ lb	squid, cleaned, cut into rings, and tentacles cut in half (calamari)	750 g
½	small bunch watercress, leaves only	½
½ lb	ITALPASTA Plain or Vegetable Wagon Wheel pasta	250 g
pinch	salt	pinch
pinch	pepper	pinch
	Romano cheese, freshly grated	

1. Preheat the oven to 400°F (200°C).
2. Bring a large pot of lightly salted water to a boil.
3. Meanwhile, heat the olive oil in a large skillet or saucepan. Add the onion and cook slowly. Add the garlic and stir. Add the olives and cook for 2 minutes. Stir in the saffron, tomato paste, wine, and fish stock. Simmer covered for 5 minutes. Add the squid and half of the watercress, stir to combine ingredients, and simmer for about 10 minutes or until the calamari is tender.
4. When the water is boiling, add the pasta and cook until *molto al dente* (very undercooked and still hard inside.) Drain the pasta well.
5. After the calamari has been simmering for about 10 minutes, stir in the pasta. Continue to cook, stirring occasionally, until the pasta is cooked through *(al dente)*.
6. Season with salt and pepper to taste and serve the pasta in soup bowls (the sauce will probably be a touch runny). Sprinkle with the Romano cheese and the remainder of the watercress.

Mezzi Rigatoni con Tonno
(MEZZI RIGATONI WITH TUNA)

Tuna is widely used in the Mediterranean areas and, like all fish and seafood, requires a minimum amoun of cooking. It is also a very tender and delicate fish, so handle with care to avoid breaking.

Makes 4 servings

2 tbsp	ITALPASTA olive oil, divided	25 mL
2 tbsp	butter, divided	25 mL
1½ lb	fresh tuna, cut into 1-inch (2.5 cm) cubes	750 g
1	medium onion, finely chopped	1
3	cloves garlic, finely chopped	3
2 tbsp	capers	25 mL
4	ITALPASTA anchovy fillets, finely diced	4
½ cup	Kalamata olives, pitted and sliced	125 mL
½ cup	white wine	125 mL
6	fresh plum tomatoes, seeded and diced	6
1 tsp	ITALPASTA tomato paste	5 mL
¼ cup	fresh parsley, finely chopped	50 mL
½ lb	ITALPASTA Mezzi Rigatoni	250 g
	fresh parsley for garnish	
½ cup	Romano cheese, freshly grated	125 mL

1. Bring a large pot of lightly salted water to a boil.
2. Meanwhile, heat 1 tbsp (15 mL) olive oil and 1 tbsp (15 mL) butter in a medium skillet and sauté the tuna over medium-high heat until it is three-quarters done (about 2 minutes). Remove from heat and, with a slotted spoo place the tuna on paper towels to absorb any fat from the pan.
3. In another large skillet, heat the remaining oil and butter. Add the onion, garlic, capers, and anchovies and sauté until the onion begins to turn golder Do not burn the garlic. Add the olives, wine, tomatoes, tomato paste, and half of the parsley, mix well and simmer for 10 minutes.
4. Meanwhile, cook the pasta *al dente* and drain well.
5. Add the tuna to the sauce and simmer for another 1 to 2 minutes, or until th tuna is cooked.
6. Add the pasta, mix thoroughly but gently, and serve with the remaining parsley and cheese.

Spaghetti con Vongole e Pomodori
(SPAGHETTI WITH A RED CLAM SAUCE)

Vongole sauce requires a long pasta like spaghetti or linguine. Most importantly, it uses a large amount of garlic. Does this mean that you are going to smell like a raw clove of garlic for the next two days? No. Cooking garlic properly, and using a lot of parsley, helps to minimize the after-effects. The garlic should also be chopped as finely as possible so that you never bite into a piece.

Makes 4 servings

METHOD 1

¼ cup	ITALPASTA olive oil	50 mL
6	cloves garlic, finely chopped	6
1	medium onion, sliced	1
2 cups	mushrooms, sliced	500 mL
1 cup	fish or chicken stock (page 123)	250 mL
2	bay leaves	2
2 cups	dry white wine	500 mL
32	small fresh clams, scrubbed well	32
2 cups	tomato sauce (page 121)	500 mL
½ lb	ITALPASTA Spaghetti	250 g
½	bunch fresh parsley with stem, very finely chopped	½
¼ cup	Parmesan cheese, freshly grated	50 mL
pinch	salt	pinch
pinch	black pepper, freshly ground	pinch

1. Bring a large pot of lightly salted water to a boil.
2. Meanwhile, in another large pot, heat the olive oil and sauté the garlic and onions.
3. Add the mushrooms and continue to sauté until the mushrooms begin to soften.
4. Add the chicken or fish stock, bay leaves, and wine and bring to a quick boil. Drop in all of the clams, cover, and simmer for 5 to 10 minutes or until the clams have opened. Discard any that stay closed. At this point, the clams should be partially cooked. (They will finish cooking in the tomato sauce.)
5. Strain the clams and put the liquid in a large skillet, reserving the clams for later use.
6. Remove the clams from the shell and add to the sauce, keeping a few for decorative purposes. (Or leave them in the shell. I prefer adding the entire clam and shell to the finished sauce for extra flavor and visual appeal.)
7. Place the skillet with the strained sauce on the stove and bring back to a boil. Let this simmer for 5 to 10 minutes or until the liquid has reduced by half.

8. Add the tomato sauce and continue to simmer slowly until it has reduced slightly. Remove the bay leaves, add the cooked clams (with or without the shells), and simmer for an additional 5 minutes or until the clams are cooked. (It doesn't take long for them to overcook and become tough.)
9. When the water has come to a boil, cook the pasta *al dente*, drain and add to the sauce along with the chopped parsley. Toss or mix well, and serve with Parmesan cheese, salt, and freshly ground black pepper.

METHOD 2

2 tbsp	ITALPASTA olive oil	25 mL
2 tbsp	butter	25 mL
1	medium onion, finely diced	1
6	cloves garlic, finely chopped	6
2 cups	mushrooms, sliced	500 mL
½ cup	dry red wine	125 mL
2 cups	plum tomatoes, peeled, seeded, and diced	500 mL
1 tsp	ITALPASTA tomato paste	5 mL
3	12-oz (375 g) tins baby clams, with juice	3
½	bunch parsley, finely chopped	½
pinch	black pepper, freshly ground	pinch
½ lb	ITALPASTA Spaghetti	250 g
¼ cup	Parmesan cheese, freshly grated	50 mL
2 tbsp	fresh parsley, chopped	25 mL

1. Bring a large pot of lightly salted water to a boil.
2. Meanwhile, in a large skillet or sauce pan, heat the olive oil and butter and sauté the onions and garlic until the onions begin to turn golden. Be careful not to burn the garlic.
3. Add the mushrooms and continue to sauté until the mushrooms begin to soften. Add the wine, tomatoes, and tomato paste. Sauté until the liquid is reduced by half.
4. Add the baby clams with juice, the parsley, and the black pepper. Simmer for about 5 minutes or until the sauce is no longer runny.
5. Meanwhile, when the water comes to a boil, add the pasta and cook *al dente*. Drain and add to the sauce. Toss or stir well and use tongs to place the pasta on a platter or in individual serving bowls. Spoon the remainder of the sauce over the top, and sprinkle with Parmesan cheese and chopped parsley.

Spaghetti con Aglio e Scampi alla Griglia

(GARLIC SPAGHETTI WITH BROILED BABY LOBSTER TAILS)

This is for that special night. A simple plate of garlic spaghetti adorned with these morsels from the sea.

Makes 2 servings

1 lb	**scampi, shell on and cut in half lengthwise**	**500 g**
pinch	**salt**	**pinch**
pinch	**pepper**	**pinch**
pinch	**paprika**	**pinch**
¼ cup	**butter**	**50 mL**
2	**cloves garlic, finely chopped**	**2**
¼ cup	**dry white wine**	**50 mL**
½	**lemon, squeezed**	**½**
1 tbsp	**fresh parsley, finely chopped**	**15 mL**
½ lb	**ITALPASTA Spaghetti**	**250 g**
2 tbsp	**additional butter**	**25 mL**
4	**additional cloves garlic, finely chopped**	**4**
¼ cup	**Parmesan cheese, freshly grated**	**50 mL**
½	**lemon, cut into wedges**	**½**
2	**sprigs fresh parsley**	**2**

1. Preheat oven to 400°F (200°C).
2. Bring a large pot of lightly salted water to a boil.
3. Meanwhile, put the scampi in a shallow casserole dish, shell-side down, and season with salt, pepper, and paprika. Put a small amount of the butter and garlic on each scampi.
4. Put casserole dish in preheated oven and bake for about 3 minutes, then broil for another 2 minutes. Remove scampi from casserole and set aside.
5. Add the wine, lemon juice, and chopped parsley to the casserole dish and simmer on the stove until mixture has reduced by half. Remove from heat. Add the scampi to the sauce.
6. Meanwhile, when the water is boiling, cook the pasta *al dente*. Drain well.
7. In a large skillet add the remaining butter and sauté garlic until golden. Shake the excess water from the pasta, add to the skillet and toss or stir well. Add the Parmesan cheese and toss or stir.
8. Arrange the pasta on a large serving dish or individual plates and arrange the scampi around the pasta with all the tails pointing to the center of the plate. Pour the sauce over the scampi, and garnish with lemon wedges and parsley sprigs. Serve immediately.

Spaghetti con Gamberi e Pomadori
(SPAGHETTI AND SHRIMP WITH A TOMATO ANCHOVY SAUCE)

The anchovy and caper flavors are captured and accentuated in the red tomato sauce. It makes for an aromatic delight.

Makes 4 servings

3 tbsp	ITALPASTA olive oil, divided	45 mL
2	cloves garlic, minced or finely chopped	2
6	ITALPASTA anchovy fillets, finely chopped	6
3 tbsp	capers	45 mL
2 cups	plum tomatoes, diced and seeded	500 mL
2 tbsp	fresh basil, chopped	25 mL
1 tsp	chili pepper flakes	5 mL
¼ tsp	salt	1 mL
¼ tsp	pepper	1 mL
1 tbsp	butter	15 mL
1½ lb	large shrimp, peeled and deveined	750 g
½ cup	red wine	125 mL
½ lb	ITALPASTA Spaghetti	250 g
	freshly grated Parmesan cheese and fresh basil leaves for garnish	

1. Bring a large pot of lightly salted water to a boil.
2. Meanwhile, in a large skillet, heat 2 tbsp (25 mL) of oil and sauté the garlic, anchovies, and capers until the garlic is sizzling but not brown. Add the tomato, basil, chili pepper flakes, salt, and pepper. Let simmer for 5 minutes.
3. In another skillet, add 1 tbsp (15 mL) oil, butter and shrimp. Sauté until shrimp begin to turn red (the shrimp should be about half cooked). Add the wine and reduce by half, about 1 minute. Add the shrimp and the reduced wine to the tomato sauce, simmer for another minute to finish cooking the shrimp. Remove from the heat while you are cooking the pasta.
4. When the water comes to a boil, add the pasta and cook *al dente*, then drain. Add the spaghetti to the shrimp sauce and return to the heat. Toss or stir well and serve garnished with Parmesan cheese and basil.

Spaghettini con Gamberi e Peperoni Arrosto

(Spaghettini with Shrimp and Roasted Bell Peppers)

Simple, quick, and to the point — but oh, so good! Although the cream is flavored with shallots and garlic, it is the nutmeg that adds the extraordinary flavor to this simple yet memorable sauce.

Makes 4 to 6 servings

3	large red bell peppers	3
2 tbsp	ITALPASTA extra virgin olive oil	25 mL
2 tbsp	butter	25 mL
4	cloves garlic, finely chopped	4
4	shallots, finely chopped	4
1½ lb	medium shrimp, peeled, deveined, and cut in half	750 g
½ cup	dry white wine	125 mL
2 tbsp	fresh parsley, finely chopped	25 mL
1 cup	whipping cream	250 mL
¼ tsp	salt	1 mL
pinch	black pepper, freshly ground	pinch
1 lb	ITALPASTA Spaghettini	500 g
¼ tsp	nutmeg	1 mL
	additional chopped parsley for garnish	

1. Roast the red peppers under the broiler or over an open flame until the skins are charred on all sides. Place them in a bowl and cover tightly with plastic wrap and let sit for about 20 minutes.
2. Bring a pot of lightly salted water to a boil.
3. Meanwhile, take the peppers out, cut them in half, remove the core, and scrape away the skin and seeds. Cut into ¼-inch (5 mm) strips and set aside.
4. Heat the oil and butter and sauté the garlic and shallots until they begin to turn a light golden color. Add the shrimp, toss or stir well, then add the wine. The heat of the pan should cause the wine to reduce immediately. Add the red peppers, chopped parsley, and cream. Season with salt, nutmeg, and pepper and simmer until the cream begins to thicken and reduce by about one quarter of its volume, about 2 minutes. (Any longer and the shrimp will be overcooked.) Remove from the heat and set aside.
5. Add the pasta to the boiling water and cook *al dente*.
6. Using a colander, drain well. Return the skillet to the heat, add the pasta, and toss or stir well. Serve at once, garnished with parsley.

Spaghetti "Rosetta" con Gamberi

(Spaghetti with Shrimp and Herbs)

The tomatoes and the cream make this sauce pink. The aromatic bouquet of the herbs will awaken your senses and bring sheer delight to your taste buds.

Makes 4 servings

3 tbsp	butter, divided	45 mL
1½ lb	medium shrimp, peeled and deveined	750 g
2 tbsp	ITALPASTA extra virgin olive oil	25 mL
1 tbsp	butter	15 mL
3	cloves garlic, finely chopped	3
1	medium leek, white and light green parts only, cut into thin slices (2 inches/5 cm)	1
2 cups	mushrooms, quartered	500 mL
2 cups	plum tomatoes, diced and seeded	500 mL
1 cup	whipping cream	250 mL
4 tbsp	fresh tarragon, chopped (or 2 tsp/10 mL dried)	50 mL
2 tbsp	fresh rosemary, chopped (or 1 tsp/5 mL dried)	25 mL
1 tsp	chervil	5 mL
¼ tsp	nutmeg	1 mL
pinch	black pepper, freshly ground	pinch
1 lb	ITALPASTA Spaghetti	500 g
1 cup	Parmesan cheese, freshly grated additional Parmesan cheese	250 mL
2 tbsp	fresh parsley, chopped	25 mL

1. Bring a large pot of lightly salted water to a boil.
2. Meanwhile, heat 2 tbsp (25 mL) of butter in a medium sized skillet and sauté the shrimp on both sides until they begin to turn red. They should be about half cooked. Remove from the heat and set aside.
3. In a large skillet, heat the oil and the remaining butter and sauté the garlic and leeks until they are clear. Add the mushrooms and continue to sauté until they begin to soften. Add the tomatoes and cream and season with the tarragon, rosemary, chervil, nutmeg, and black pepper. Stir well with a wooden spoon and let simmer for 10 minutes or until the sauce begins to thicken.
4. When the water comes to a boil, cook the pasta *al dente*. Drain well.
5. When the sauce is slightly thickened, add the partially cooked shrimp and cook for about 1 minute or until the shrimp is done.
6. Add the pasta to the sauce. Add the Parmesan cheese, toss or stir well, and put the pasta onto a large serving dish or individual plates. Pour the seafood and sauce over top and garnish with additional Parmesan cheese and parsley.

Spaghettini con Frutti di Mare e Pomodori

(SPAGHETTINI WITH SQUID AND SHRIMP IN A SPICY TOMATO SAUCE)

A lightly spicy tomato sauce, combined with the delicacies of the ocean and fine pasta, makes this an exemplary Southern Italian dish.

Makes 4 servings

½ lb	**ITALPASTA Spaghettini**	250 g
2 tbsp	**butter**	25 mL
1 tbsp	**ITALPASTA olive oil**	15 mL
1	**medium onion, finely diced**	1
4	**cloves garlic, finely minced**	4
½ lb	**squid, cleaned and thinly sliced**	250 g
1 tsp	**oregano**	5 mL
1 tsp	**rosemary**	5 mL
1 tsp	**chili pepper flakes (more if desired)**	5 mL
pinch	**salt**	pinch
pinch	**pepper**	pinch
½ cup	**dry red wine**	125 mL
½ cup	**chicken stock (page 123)**	125 mL
1	**ITALPASTA 28-oz (796 mL) tin plum tomatoes, finely diced with the juice**	1
1 lb	**medium shrimp, peeled and deveined**	500 g
¼ cup	**Parmesan cheese, freshly grated**	50 mL

Bring a large pot of lightly salted water to a boil and cook the pasta *al dente*. Drain and set aside.

Heat the butter and oil in a large saucepan and sauté the onion and garlic over medium heat until the onion begins to turn golden.

Add the squid, oregano, rosemary, chili pepper flakes, salt, and pepper, and continue to sauté, tossing or stirring frequently until the squid begins to get firm, about 1 minute.

Add the wine and chicken stock and reduce by half. Add the tomatoes and bring to a boil. Let simmer for 8 to 10 minutes or until the sauce begins to thicken. Add the shrimp and continue to simmer for 2 minutes or until the shrimp are cooked.

Add the pasta, toss or stir well, making sure the pasta is hot. Serve immediately sprinkled with Parmesan cheese.

Spaghettini con Salsa di Lumache e Acciughe

(SPAGHETTINI WITH SNAILS AND ANCHOVY SAUCE)

I have always loved escargot. A single topping of butter and garlic would be enough to put me in heaven. Here is a recipe with a few more ingredients. It's just as quick and easy to prepare and offers flavors that will delight your taste buds.

Makes 4 to 6 servings

1 lb	**ITALPASTA Spaghettini**	500 g
1 tbsp	**ITALPASTA olive oil**	15 mL
1 tbsp	**butter**	15 mL
1	**medium onion, diced**	1
3	**cloves garlic, finely chopped**	3
1	**14-oz (400 g) tin snails, drained**	1
15	**ITALPASTA anchovies, mashed and chopped with their oil**	15
½ cup	**white wine**	125 mL
pinch	**chili pepper flakes**	pinch
2	**sprigs basil, diced**	2
½ tsp	**oregano**	2 mL
4	**fresh plum tomatoes, peeled, seeded, and chopped**	4
3 tbsp	**fresh parsley, chopped**	45 mL
	Parmesan cheese, freshly grated	

1. Bring a large pot of lightly salted water to a boil. Cook the pasta *al dente* and drain.
2. Heat the oil and butter in a large frying pan and sauté the onion and garlic until they begin to brown.
3. Add the snails and the anchovies. Stir and add all remaining ingredients except the parsley and cheese. Stir well and simmer for about 5 minutes, stirring frequently.
4. Add the cooked pasta and parsley and toss or stir well.
5. Serve immediately with a light sprinkle of Parmesan cheese.

Penne al Limone con Pesce

(PENNE WITH SEA BASS AND MUSSELS IN A LEMON CREAM SAUCE)

Myriad ingredients make this a wonderfully flavored sauce that's quick to cook. Make sure to have plenty of crusty Italian bread — you will need it to wipe the plate clean.

Makes 4 servings

1 tbsp	ITALPASTA extra virgin olive oil, divided	15 mL
1 tbsp	butter, divided	15 mL
1½ lb	fillet of sea bass, cut into ½-inch (1 cm) pieces (red snapper can also be used)	750 g
pinch	salt	pinch
pinch	pepper, freshly ground	pinch
1	medium onion, finely diced	1
4	cloves of garlic, finely chopped	4
¼ cup	sun-dried tomatoes, julienne*	50 mL
½ cup	dry white wine	125 mL
1 cup	whipping cream	250 mL
¼ tsp	nutmeg	1 mL
1 tbsp	fresh rosemary	15 mL
1 tbsp	lemon juice	15 mL
pinch	salt	pinch
pinch	pepper, freshly ground	pinch
20	cultured mussels	20
1	sweet red bell pepper, julienne	1
½ lb	ITALPASTA Plain or Vegetable Penne Rigate	250 g
¼ cup	freshly grated Parmesan cheese	50 mL
	additional Parmesan cheese	
2 tbsp	fresh parsley, chopped	25 mL

Julienne is strips 2 inches (5 cm) long by ¼ inch (5 mm) wide

1. Bring a pot of lightly salted water to a boil.
2. Meanwhile, put the olive oil and half of the butter in a medium-sized skillet. Season the sea bass with salt and pepper and pan-fry the strips until they are brown on both sides. Make sure that the fish is completely cooked and, using a slotted spoon, transfer it onto a paper or cloth towel to absorb the oil.
3. In another large skillet, use the remainder of the oil and butter to sauté the onion and garlic until the onion is clear, taking care not to burn the garlic. Add the sun-dried tomatoes, reduce the heat to medium-low and continue to sauté until the tomatoes begin to soften, about 2 to 3 minutes.
4. Add the wine, increase the heat to medium, and continue to cook until mixture is reduced by half. Add the cream, nutmeg, rosemary, lemon juice, salt, and pepper, and bring to a boil, stirring constantly so the cream does not burn.
5. Reduce the heat and add the mussels and red pepper. Cover and simmer for about 5 minutes or until the mussels have opened. Discard any that have not opened. Remove from heat, place the cooked sea bass on top of the mixture, cover and set aside.
6. When the water is boiling, cook the pasta *al dente*, drain well and place in a mixing bowl. Add the Parmesan cheese and mix well. Transfer the pasta to a serving platter or individual plates. Spoon the seafood and sauce over the pasta, taking care not to break the sea bass. Sprinkle with additional Parmesan cheese and parsley and serve.

Spaghettini con Gamberoni e Aglio
(SPAGHETTINI WITH SHRIMP, GARLIC, AND BUTTER)

...s of garlic, butter, and shrimp; a delicate pasta to take in all the flavors; a little white wine and ...rmesan cheese. Voilà. What more could one ask?

...kes 4 to 6 servings

1 lb	ITALPASTA Spaghettini	500 g
3 tbsp	butter	45 mL
1 tbsp	ITALPASTA extra virgin olive oil	15 mL
6	shallots, finely chopped	6
6	cloves garlic, finely chopped	6
2 lb	large shrimp, peeled and deveined	1 kg
pinch	salt	pinch
pinch	pepper	pinch
½ tsp	crushed chili peppers	2 mL
2 tbsp	lemon juice	25 mL
1 cup	dry white wine	250 mL
½ cup	Parmesan cheese, freshly grated	125 mL
¼ cup	fresh parsley, chopped	50 mL

Bring a large pot of lightly salted water to a boil.

Meanwhile, heat the butter and oil in a large skillet or frying pan and sauté the shallots and garlic.

Add the shrimp, salt, pepper, and chili peppers and continue to cook until the shrimp begin to turn pink. Toss or stir frequently so that the garlic does not burn.

Add the lemon juice and white wine. Continue to cook over medium-high heat until the shrimp is cooked and the wine is reduced. Remove from the heat and set aside.

Add pasta to the boiling water and cook *al dente*. Drain well.

Return the shrimp to the stove and add the pasta, Parmesan cheese, and parsley. Toss or stir well and serve with crusty Italian bread.

Spaghettini al Tonno Fresco
(SPAGHETTINI WITH FRESH TUNA AND RED BELL PEPPERS)

A reminder: Tuna is a very delicate fish. It might flake when it is raw and definitely will when it is cooked. A subtle and unmistakable flavor, combined with herbs and garlic, makes this meal well worth the care you will put into it.

Makes 4 to 6 servings

4	red bell peppers	4
1 lb	ITALPASTA Spaghettini	500 g
3 tbsp	ITALPASTA extra virgin olive oil	45 mL
4	cloves garlic, finely chopped	4
1	medium onion, thinly sliced	1
1½ lb	fresh tuna, chopped into ½-inch (1 cm) chunks	750 g
¼ tsp	salt	1 mL
pinch	black pepper, freshly ground	pinch
2 tbsp	fresh rosemary	25 mL
1 tbsp	fresh thyme	15 mL
1 cup	dry white wine, divided	250 mL
3 tbsp	capers	45 mL
2 tbsp	lemon juice	25 mL
2 tbsp	fresh parsley, finely chopped	25 mL

1. Bring a pot of lightly salted water to a boil.
2. Roast the red peppers under the broiler or over an open flame until the skin is charred on all sides. Put them in a bowl and cover tightly with plastic wrap for about 15 to 20 minutes.
3. Meanwhile, add pasta to the boiling water and cook *al dente*.
4. Put the olive oil in a large skillet and, over medium heat, sauté garlic and onion until the onion begins to turn golden. (Do not let the garlic burn.)
5. Season the tuna with salt and freshly ground black pepper and add it to the pan. Add the rosemary, thyme, and ½ cup (125 mL) of the wine. Increase the heat to about medium-high and cook until the tuna is brown.
6. Cut roasted red peppers in half, remove the core, seeds, and skin. Cut into julienne strips about 2 inches (5 cm) by ¼ inch (5 mm).
7. Add the roasted peppers, capers, and lemon juice to the tuna and cook for another minute, stirring often and gently until the tuna is cooked. Remove from heat.
8. Return the saucepan to the stove and, over medium-high heat, add the remaining wine to the pan. It will reduce immediately. Drain and add the pasta to the pan, toss or stir well, and serve immediately sprinkled with parsley.

CHAPTER TWO

Pasta with Vegetables

Eating all your vegetables can be a sensuous pleasure

when you combine them with pasta. Imagine sweet,

sun-soaked tomatoes, tender green zucchini, deep purple

eggplant, fleshy brown mushrooms and pale green

artichokes. Combine and cook them carefully to take

full advantage of the flavor, texture, and color unique

to each. Add fresh herbs, fruity olive oil, a delicate sauce

and enjoy!

Conchiglie in Brodo con Patate

(PASTA SHELLS AND POTATOES IN BROTH)

A soup-like entrée perfect for a hearty and healthy lunch on a cold winter day.

Makes 4 to 6 servings

1 tbsp	butter	15 mL
1 tbsp	ITALPASTA olive oil	15 mL
3-4	medium shallots	3-4
2	celery stalks, diced	2
3	medium carrots, diced	3
6	medium potatoes, diced	6
2 tbsp	fresh basil, finely chopped	25 mL
1 tbsp	fresh thyme, coarsely chopped	15 mL
2 cups	chicken stock (page 123)	500 mL
1 tbsp	ITALPASTA tomato paste	15 mL
2 tbsp	fresh parsley, finely chopped	25 mL
¼ tsp	salt	1 mL
pinch	pepper	pinch
1 lb	ITALPASTA Shells	500 g
2 tbsp	pecorino cheese, freshly grated	25 mL
2 tbsp	Parmesan cheese, freshly grated	25 mL

1. Heat the butter and oil in a large saucepan and sauté the shallots, celery, and carrots over medium heat until the shallots become soft. Add the potatoes, basil, and thyme and continue to sauté for 1 or 2 minutes, stirring or tossing often so as not to burn the shallots.
2. Add the chicken stock and tomato paste and stir well. Add the parsley, salt, and pepper. Bring to a boil then reduce the heat and let simmer for about 20 to 30 minutes.
3. While this is simmering, bring a large pot of lightly salted water to a boil and cook the pasta slightly less than *al dente*. Drain and add to the broth. Simmer for an additional 3 to 5 minutes. Taste for seasoning and serve sprinkled with the grated cheeses.

Farfalle con Funghi e Marsala

(BOW TIES WITH WILD MUSHROOMS IN A MARSALA WINE SAUCE)

Marsala wine is commonly used with veal and pork. Although you can use a dry Marsala, I just love the way meaty wild mushrooms absorb the sweetness of this wine.

Makes 4 to 6 servings

2 tbsp	butter	25 mL
2 tbsp	ITALPASTA extra virgin olive oil	25 mL
3	shallots, finely chopped	3
3	cloves garlic, finely chopped (more or less to taste)	3
1½ cups	cremini mushrooms, sliced	375 mL
1½ cups	oyster mushrooms, sliced	375 mL
1½ cups	shiitake mushrooms, sliced	375 mL
1½ cups	portobello mushrooms, sliced the same size as the other mushrooms	375 mL
¼ tsp	salt	1 mL
pinch	black pepper, freshly ground	pinch
1 cup	sweet Marsala wine	250 mL
1½ cups	whipping cream	375 mL
¼ cup	Parmesan cheese, freshly grated	50 mL
¼ tsp	nutmeg	1 mL
1 lb	ITALPASTA Bow Ties or Vegetable Bow Ties	500 g
2 tbsp	fresh parsley, finely chopped	25 mL
1 tbsp	Parmesan cheese for garnish	15 mL

1. Bring a pot of lightly salted water to a boil.
2. Meanwhile, put the butter and oil in a large skillet and, over medium heat, sauté the shallots and garlic. Add the mushrooms and season with salt and black pepper. Continue to sauté until the mushrooms have softened considerably and most of the liquid has evaporated. Stir or toss often to avoid burning the garlic.
3. Add the wine and continue to cook until the liquid is reduced by a third.
4. Add the cream, Parmesan cheese, and nutmeg. Stir well and continue to cook until the sauce begins to thicken. Check for seasoning, then remove from heat and set aside.
5. When the water comes to a boil, add the pasta and cook *al dente*. Drain well, then return the sauce to the stove. Bring the sauce back to a boil, then add the pasta. Stir or toss well and serve with parsley and freshly grated Parmesan cheese.

Paglia e Fieno con Piselli e Funghi

(YELLOW AND GREEN EGG FETTUCCINE WITH PEAS AND MUSHROOMS)

Wild mushrooms and prosciutto blend to give cream a unique flavor that the colored egg noodles drink up. Add the cheese... well, you be the judge.

Makes 4 to 6 servings

1 lb	ITALPASTA Paglia e Fieno or ITALPASTA Egg Fettuccine (both are egg noodles)	500 g
1 lb	frozen tiny peas, thawed (or fresh shelled peas)	500 g
4 cups	oyster mushrooms, cut in half	1 L
3 tbsp	butter	45 mL
1 tbsp	ITALPASTA extra virgin olive oil	15 mL
1	medium sweet onion, finely diced	1
6 oz	prosciutto ham cut into thin strips, ¼-inch (5 mm) pieces	175 g
pinch	salt	pinch
pinch	black pepper, freshly ground	pinch
1½ cups	whipping cream	375 mL
¼ cup	Parmesan cheese, freshly grated	50 mL
¼ cup	Romano cheese, freshly grated	50 mL
1	small sweet red pepper, seeded and finely chopped	1

1. Bring a pot of lightly salted water to a boil.
2. Boil peas until tender. Drain and set aside.
3. In a large skillet, add the butter and oil, and sauté the onions and prosciutto until the onions have softened.
4. Add the mushrooms and continue to sauté, stirring often until the mushrooms begin to soften.
5. Add the cream, salt, pepper, and the two cheeses. Stir in the cheeses so that there are no lumps and simmer until the sauce thickens.
6. When the water is at a boil, cook the pasta *al dente*, drain, and add to the sauce along with the cooked peas. Toss well and serve sprinkled with the diced red peppers.

Linguine con Pesto di Kalamata

(LINGUINE WITH BLACK OLIVE PESTO)

For the olive lover, here is a different version of the traditional basil pesto. Make this sauce a day prior serving to let the flavors mature.

Makes 4 servings

2 cups	pitted Kalamata olives	500 mL
⅓ cup	fresh basil leaves	75 mL
⅓ cup	pine nuts	75 mL
3	cloves garlic, finely minced	3
2 tbsp	lemon juice	25 mL
¾ cup	ITALPASTA extra virgin olive oil	175 mL
2 tbsp	butter	25 mL
1	medium sweet red pepper, diced	1
1	medium sweet yellow pepper, diced	1
1 lb	ITALPASTA Linguine	500 g
¼ cup	pecorino cheese, freshly grated	50 mL

1. Bring a pot of lightly salted water to a boil.
2. Place the olives, basil, pine nuts, garlic, and lemon juice in a food processor and blend until smooth. Pour the oil slowly into the food processor until it is well blended with the olive purée.
3. Heat the butter in a large skillet and sauté the peppers for about 1 minute or until they are heated through. They should be very crunchy. Add the olive pesto, mix well and set aside.
4. When the water comes to a boil, add the pasta and cook *al dente*. Drain well and add to the pesto. Return to the stove and cook just to heat through, then serve liberally sprinkled with the pecorino cheese.

Penne alla Rustica
(PENNE WITH WILD MUSHROOMS AND GREEN PEPPER)

This is a simple recipe that I have adapted to take advantage of the easy availability of wild and exotic mushrooms.

Makes 4 to 6 servings

12 oz	**ITALPASTA Penne**	375 g
2 tbsp	**butter**	25 mL
1	**medium onion, julienne***	1
3	**cloves garlic, chopped**	3
1 cup	**portobello mushrooms, sliced**	250 mL
1 cup	**oyster mushrooms, sliced**	250 mL
1 cup	**shiitake mushrooms, sliced**	250 mL
2	**green peppers, julienne**	2
½ cup	**peas**	125 mL
½ cup	**black olives, pitted and cut in half**	125 mL
1½ cups	**tomato sauce (page 121)**	375 mL
pinch	**salt**	pinch
pinch	**pepper**	pinch
¼ cup	**Parmesan cheese, freshly grated**	50 mL

Julienne is strips 2 inches (5 cm) long by ¼ inch (5 mm) wide

1. In a large pot of lightly salted water, cook the penne *al dente*. Drain and set aside.
2. Heat the butter in a frying pan and sauté the onion, garlic, and mushrooms until the mushrooms are tender.
3. Add the green peppers, peas, and black olives. Toss or stir, add the tomato sauce and simmer for about 3 to 5 minutes.
4. Add the cooked pasta to the tomato sauce. Add salt and pepper. Toss well and simmer for 1 minute. Spoon the pasta onto a large serving dish or individual plates and pour the remaining sauce over the pasta. Sprinkle with Parmesan cheese and serve at once.

Penne di Maresciallo
(PENNE WITH ASPARAGUS AND HAM)

This recipe comes from a chef who learned it in his home town in Italy. It was shown to him by the T[...] Marshal (Maresciallo), who spent most of his time cooking.

Makes 4 to 6 servings

3 tbsp	**butter**	45 mL
1	**medium onion, julienne***	1
3	**cloves garlic, finely chopped**	3
¼ lb	**cooked ham**	125 g
1 lb	**asparagus, cut into 1-inch pieces, cooked but crunchy and rinsed in cold water**	500 g
1	**yellow pepper, julienne**	1
1	**sweet red pepper, julienne**	1
½ cup	**dry white wine**	125 mL
1 lb	**ITALPASTA Penne**	500 g
¼ tsp	**salt**	1 mL
pinch	**pepper**	pinch
½ cup	**Parmesan cheese, freshly grated**	125 mL
¼ cup	**Romano cheese, freshly grated**	50 mL
¼ cup	**additional Parmesan cheese chopped parsley, for garnish**	50 mL

Julienne is strips 2 inches (5 cm) long by ¼ inch (5 mm) wide

1. Bring a large pot of lightly salted water to a boil.
2. In a large frying pan, heat the butter and sauté the onion, garlic, and ham until the ham browns slightly but the onion and garlic remain clear.
3. Add the asparagus and peppers and continue to sauté, tossing or stirring frequently for about 1 to 2 minutes.
4. Add the wine and allow it to reduce by half.
5. When the water comes to a boil, cook the pasta *al dente*, drain well, then a[dd] the pasta to the pan. Add salt and pepper. Toss or stir well and cook for 1 t[o] 2 minutes, or until all the ingredients are hot.
6. Add the Parmesan and Romano cheeses and stir well. Serve immediately garnished with extra cheese and parsley.

Rotini con Carciofi
(ROTINI WITH ARTICHOKE HEARTS)

Some say that scallops are treasures of the sea. I feel that artichokes are treasures of the land. Hidden by their rough exterior, the hearts are a true find.

Makes 4 servings

1 tbsp	**ITALPASTA olive oil**	15 mL
1 tbsp	**butter**	25 mL
1	**medium onion, diced**	1
3	**cloves garlic, chopped**	3
1	**stalk celery, diced**	1
½ cup	**sun-dried tomatoes, julienne***	125 mL
½ cup	**sherry or white wine**	125 mL
¼ cup	**brandy**	50 mL
1 cup	**chicken stock (page 123)**	250 mL
2 tbsp	**ITALPASTA tomato paste**	25 mL
3 tbsp	**fresh basil, chopped**	45 mL
pinch	**chili pepper**	pinch
1	**14-oz (398 mL) tin artichoke hearts, drained and quartered**	1
½ lb	**ITALPASTA Rotini**	250 g
¼ cup	**Parmesan cheese, freshly grated**	50 mL

Julienne is strips 2 inches (5 cm) long by ¼ inch (5 mm) wide

1. Heat the oil and butter in a frying pan. Sauté the onion, garlic, and celery for 2 to 3 minutes or until golden. Add the sun-dried tomatoes and continue to cook over medium-low heat for 2 to 3 minutes, or until the tomatoes begin to soften. Add wine, brandy, chicken stock, tomato paste, basil, and chili pepper and simmer for about 15 minutes.
2. Add the artichoke hearts and simmer for another 1 to 2 minutes.
3. Bring a pot of lightly salted water to a boil, cook the pasta *al dente*, and drain.
4. Add the pasta to the sauce and toss or stir well. Check for seasoning and serve with freshly grated Parmesan cheese.

Rotini alla Fiorentina con Pinoli

(PASTA WITH SPINACH AND PINE NUTS)

The gentle flavor and soft texture of pine nuts make them a wonderful addition to many recipes. Here is one that includes spinach and rotini.

Makes 4 to 6 servings

2 tbsp	ITALPASTA olive oil	25 mL
2 tbsp	butter	25 mL
¼ lb	pancetta (salted, raw pork belly) diced into ¼-inch (5 mm) pieces	125 g
2	cloves garlic, finely chopped	2
4	green onions, chopped	4
¾ lb	spinach (stems removed and leaves cut in half)	375 g
1 lb	ITALPASTA Rotini	500 g
1 cup	pine nuts, lightly toasted	250 mL
¼ cup	Parmesan cheese, freshly grated	50 mL
¼ cup	chicken stock (page 123)	50 mL
pinch	salt	pinch
pinch	pepper	pinch
	additional Parmesan cheese, freshly grated	

1. Heat oil and butter in a pan and sauté the pancetta until it is brown. Add the garlic and onions and sauté until tender.
2. Add the spinach and continue to sauté over low heat until it wilts, but retains its flavor.
3. Bring a pot of lightly salted water to a boil, cook the pasta *al dente* and drain.
4. Add the pasta to the pan along with half of the pine nuts, ¼ cup (50 mL) of Parmesan cheese, all the chicken stock, salt, and pepper.
5. Divide into portions and sprinkle with the remaining pine nuts and a dusting of Parmesan cheese.

...otini con Broccoletti

(...TINI WITH BROCCOLI AND ANCHOVY)

...n all recipes, it is the combination of ingredients that creates a particular taste. In this recipe, anchovy, ...c, and chili peppers blend for a subtle flavor.

...es 4 to 6 servings

2 tbsp	ITALPASTA olive oil	25 mL
1	medium onion, chopped	1
3	cloves garlic, minced	3
3 oz	pancetta or bacon, chopped	90 g
6	anchovies, very finely chopped	6
1 lb	broccoli, cut into small florets with stalk peeled and diced	500 g
2	sweet red peppers, julienne*	2
pinch	salt	pinch
pinch	pepper	pinch
¼ tsp	chili pepper, crushed	1 mL
¼ cup	Parmesan cheese, freshly grated	50 mL
1 lb	ITALPASTA Rotini	500 g
	additional Parmesan cheese, freshly grated	

Julienne is strips 2 inches (5 cm) long by ¼ inch (5 mm) wide

Cook the broccoli in boiling salted water. Rinse under cold water and then drain.

Heat the oil in a large frying pan and sauté the onion, garlic, and pancetta until the pancetta is lightly browned and the onion and garlic remain clear. Add the anchovies, broccoli, red peppers, salt, pepper, and chili pepper and toss well. Sauté for 1 to 2 minutes or until all the ingredients are hot. Meanwhile, bring a large pot of lightly salted water to a boil and cook the pasta *al dente*. Drain and add the pasta to the frying pan. Add the Parmesan cheese, toss or stir well, and cook for about 1 minute.

Serve immediately with additional Parmesan cheese.

Fusilli e Insalata Tricolore

(SAUTÉ OF TRI-COLORED LETTUCE AND FUSILLI)

If you think that lettuce is only to be eaten raw and in salads, here is a refreshing change. These meatier lettuces take well to a quick sauté and remain crunchy and very flavorful. Red cabbage can also be added to this colorful dish.

Makes 4 servings

1	medium head radicchio, cleaned and trimmed into ½-inch (1 cm) strips	1
2	heads Belgian endive, sliced across their width into ½-inch (1 cm) strips	2
5 cups	arugula, cleaned and coarsely chopped	1.25 L
¼ cup	ITALPASTA extra virgin olive oil	50 mL
3 tsp	garlic, finely chopped	15 mL
½ tsp	red chili peppers, crushed	2 mL
¼ tsp	salt	1 mL
pinch	black pepper, freshly ground	pinch
1 lb	ITALPASTA Vegetable Fusilli	500 g
½ cup	Romano cheese, freshly grated	125 mL

1. Bring a large pot of lightly salted water to a boil.
2. Combine the radicchio, endive, and arugula in a large mixing bowl.
3. Heat the olive oil in a very large skillet and sauté the garlic and the red chili pepper for about 1 minute. Do not let the garlic burn. Add the sliced lettuce and season with salt and pepper. Sauté over medium-high heat, tossing continuously until the lettuce begins to wilt but remains crunchy, about 2 to 3 minutes.
4. When the water is boiling, add the pasta and cook *al dente*. Drain and add to the vegetables. Add the grated cheese, toss well, and serve hot or at room temperature.

Spaghetti all'Amatriciana

(SPAGHETTI WITH TOMATOES, ONION, HAM, AND CHEESE)

Amatriciana is a dish one would find in country homes. Here is just one version of this zesty meal.

Makes 4 to 6 servings

1 lb	ITALPASTA Spaghetti	500 g
1 tbsp	butter	15 mL
1 tbsp	ITALPASTA olive oil	15 mL
1	medium onion, diced	1
3	cloves garlic, finely chopped	3
¼ lb	pancetta or prosciutto, finely diced	125 g
¼ cup	dry red wine	50 mL
4	plum tomatoes, peeled and seeded	4
pinch	black pepper, freshly ground	pinch
¼ tsp	chili peppers, crushed	1 mL
dash	Tabasco sauce	dash
¼ cup	pecorino cheese, coarsely grated	50 mL
¼ cup	Romano cheese, coarsely grated	50 mL

1. Cook the pasta in lightly salted boiling water *al dente*. Drain, and set aside. Have a large pot of water on the stove simmering to complete the pasta.
2. In a large skillet, sauté the onion and garlic in the butter and oil until clear.
3. Add the prosciutto or pancetta and continue to sauté until the ham begins to brown, about 2 to 3 minutes.
4. Add the wine and then the tomatoes to the pan. Stir well and season with freshly ground black pepper, chili peppers, and Tabasco. (Do not use salt, as the ham is already salty.) Let simmer for 2 to 3 minutes.
5. Put the pasta in a large strainer and immerse in the simmering water for 10 seconds. Shake off the excess water and add the pasta to the sauce. Toss well and serve immediately sprinkled with pecorino and Romano cheeses.

Spaghettini alla Checca

(SPAGHETTINI WITH FRESH TOMATOES, HERBS, AND MOZZARELLA)

Prepared with an uncooked sauce, this dish is brimming with flavor and ideal for a summer lunch or dinner.

Makes 4 to 6 servings

3 lb	fresh plum tomatoes, peeled, seeded, and diced into ¼-inch (5 mm) pieces	1.5 kg
½ lb	whole milk Italian mozzarella, diced into ¼-inch (5 mm) pieces	250 g
2 tbsp	fresh basil, chopped	25 mL
2 tbsp	fresh oregano, chopped	25 mL
2 tbsp	marjoram, chopped	25 mL
1 tbsp	fresh thyme, chopped	15 mL
pinch	salt	pinch
pinch	pepper	pinch
½ cup	ITALPASTA extra virgin olive oil	125 mL
1 lb	ITALPASTA Spaghettini	500 g

1. Bring a pot of lightly salted water to a boil.
2. Put the tomatoes, mozzarella, and all of the herbs in a large mixing bowl that will be large enough to hold the pasta. Season with salt and pepper and mix well.
3. Heat the olive oil in a skillet, pour it over the vegetables, and mix well.
4. When the water is boiling, cook the pasta *al dente*. Drain well, and add to the vegetable mixture. Toss or stir well, until the pasta is coated with the oil and herbs. Cover the bowl and let stand for about 2 minutes (until the cheese begins to melt), then serve.

Fettuccine Primavera alla Panna
(FETTUCCINE WITH FRESH VEGETABLES IN A CREAM SAUCE)

...avera is found in most Italian restaurants. Every restaurant and every chef will have a different recipe ... style, but the common factor is the use of fresh vegetables and pasta. A cream sauce or tomato sauce ... be used.

...kes 4 to 6 servings

3 tbsp	butter	45 mL
1	large onion, diced	1
½ lb	mushrooms, sliced	250 g
3	large carrots, ¼-inch (5 mm) slices, cooked but crunchy and refreshed in cold water	3
1	large red pepper, julienne*	1
2	bunches broccoli florets, cooked but crunchy and refreshed in cold water	2
½	head cauliflower florets, cooked but crunchy and refreshed in cold water	½
1	bunch asparagus, cut into 1-inch (2.5 cm) pieces	1
1½ cups	whipping cream	375 mL
½ cup	Parmesan cheese, freshly grated	125 mL
pinch	salt	pinch
pinch	white pepper	pinch
¼ tsp	nutmeg	1 mL
2 tbsp	fresh parsley, chopped	25 mL
1 lb	ITALPASTA Fettuccine	500 g
¼ cup	additional Parmesan cheese, freshly grated	50 mL

*Julienne is strips 2 inches (5 cm) long by ¼ inch (5 mm) wide

Heat the butter in a large frying pan. Add the onion and mushrooms and sauté until tender. Add the carrots, red peppers, broccoli, cauliflower, and asparagus and continue to sauté. Toss or stir frequently until the vegetables are heated, about 3 to 5 minutes over medium heat.

Add the cream and Parmesan cheese and whip until the cheese is blended. Add salt, pepper, and nutmeg and simmer until the sauce has thickened slightly. Do not overcook the vegetables while the sauce is simmering. Meanwhile, bring a large pot of lightly salted water to a boil and cook the pasta *al dente*. Drain and add the pasta to the sauce. Toss or stir. Fork the pasta onto individual plates or a large serving platter. Spoon the sauce and vegetables over the pasta, and sprinkle with extra Parmesan cheese and chopped parsley. Serve immediately.

Fettuccine a Nidi con Asparagi e Basilico
(MEDIUM NEST FETTUCCINE WITH ASPARAGUS AND BASIL)

There is nothing like fresh asparagus and fresh basil combined with pasta and tomatoes. This makes an excellent and colorful meal. When asparagus is in season, you can't ask for anything more.

Makes 4 servings

2 tbsp	ITALPASTA extra virgin olive oil	25 mL
4 tbsp	butter, divided	50 mL
2 lb	fresh asparagus spears, thicker ones preferred	1 kg
4	cloves garlic, finely chopped (more or less to taste)	4
3	large shallots, finely chopped	3
½ tsp	chili peppers, crushed	2 mL
½ cup	fresh basil leaves, roughly cut	125 mL
6	large plum tomatoes, peeled, seeded, and diced	6
pinch	salt	pinch
pinch	pepper	pinch
1 cup	chicken stock (page 123)	250 mL
¾ lb	ITALPASTA Medium Nest Pasta	375 g
½ cup	Parmesan cheese, freshly grated	125 mL
2 tbsp	additional basil, chopped	25 mL
2 tbsp	fresh parsley, chopped	25 mL

1. Cut the woody bottoms off the asparagus and cut the spears diagonally into slices about an inch long, making sure the heads are left whole.
2. Bring a large pot of lightly salted water to a boil.
3. While the water is coming to a boil, put the oil and half of the butter in a large saucepan or skillet over medium heat, and sauté the asparagus pieces for about 1 minute. Add the garlic, shallots, chili pepper, and basil and continue to sauté for about 2 minutes, tossing frequently.
4. Add the diced tomatoes, salt, and pepper and mix well. Add the chicken stock and let simmer for no more than 3 minutes. (You do not want to overcook the asparagus and lose the color of the tomatoes.)
5. While this is simmering (or if it is done, remove from the heat), add the pasta to the boiling water and cook *al dente*. Drain well and add the pasta to the sauce. Add the Parmesan cheese and additional basil, toss or stir well, and serve. Place a serving of the pasta in a bowl and spoon the asparagus mixture and some of the juice on top. Sprinkle with fresh parsley.

Tagliatelle al Radicchio e Indivia del Belgio

(TAGLIATELLE [EGG FETTUCCINE] WITH RADICCHIO, BELGIAN ENDIVE, AND SUN-DRIED TOMATOES)

The texture of the radicchio and endive make them ideal for dishes other than salads. Try this with egg noodles and poached lettuce.

Makes 4 to 6 servings

1 tbsp	vegetable oil	15 mL
2 tbsp	butter	25 mL
1	medium sweet onion, finely chopped	1
⅓ lb	pancetta or bacon, cut into ¼-inch wide strips	170 g
½ cup	sun-dried tomatoes, thinly sliced	125 mL
½ cup	dry white wine	125 mL
1 lb	radicchio, shredded	500 g
1 lb	Belgian endive, shredded	500 g
1 cup	whipping cream	250 mL
pinch	nutmeg	pinch
2 tbsp	fresh parsley, chopped	25 mL
pinch	salt	pinch
pinch	pepper	pinch
1 lb	ITALPASTA Egg Fettuccine	500 g
½ cup	Parmesan cheese, freshly grated	125 mL

1. Bring a large pot of lightly salted water to a boil.
2. Heat the oil and butter in a large skillet. Sauté onion and pancetta until the pancetta is crispy and the onion is golden.
3. Add the tomatoes and sauté for another minute until they begin to soften. Add the wine and simmer until most of the wine is reduced.
4. Add the radicchio and endive, toss or stir well. Reduce heat, cover, and let simmer, stirring occasionally until the radicchio and endive wilt and have a creamy texture, about 5 minutes.
5. Remove the lid, increase the heat, and continue to cook until almost all the liquid has evaporated. Add the cream and nutmeg and cook, stirring frequently, until the sauce is reduced slightly. Stir in the parsley and remove from the heat.
6. When the water has boiled, add the pasta and cook *al dente*.
7. Return the pan to the stove, drain the pasta, and add it to the pan with the grated cheese. Toss well and serve.

Tagliatelle con Ceci

(TAGLIATELLE [EGG FETTUCCINE] WITH CHICKPEAS AND TOMATOES)

I love chickpeas covered in generous helpings of freshly ground black pepper. Here is a simple and light dish with a slight aroma of rosemary.

Makes 4 servings

1 tbsp	butter	15 mL
2 tbsp	ITALPASTA extra virgin olive oil	25 mL
¾ cup	yellow onion, finely chopped	175 mL
3	cloves garlic, finely chopped	3
1	ITALPASTA 19-oz (540 mL) tin plum tomatoes, cut, seeds removed, and the juice kept	1
3 tbsp	fresh rosemary, finely chopped	45 mL
pinch	salt	pinch
pinch	black pepper, freshly ground	pinch
2 cups	ITALPASTA canned chickpeas, drained	500 mL
½ cup	Parmesan cheese, freshly grated	125 mL
¼ cup	dry red wine	50 mL
1 lb	ITALPASTA Egg Noodles	500 g
2 tbsp	chives, chopped	25 mL

1. Bring a large pot of lightly salted water to a boil.
2. Heat the butter and oil in a large skillet and sauté the onions until a light golden color. Add the garlic and when it begins to sweat, add the tomatoes and rosemary. Season with salt and pepper and simmer for about 15 minutes or until most of the tomato liquid is reduced.
3. Add the chickpeas and continue to simmer for another 5 minutes.
4. Using a slotted spoon, remove about one third of the chickpeas. Mash them with a fork or put them through a food processor. Return chickpeas to pan with half of the Parmesan cheese and the red wine. Simmer for another 2 to 3 minutes.
5. When the water is boiling, add the pasta and cook *al dente*. Drain well and add to the sauce. Toss and serve with the remaining Parmesan cheese and chives as garnish.

CHAPTER THREE

Pasta with Meat & Poultry

Marry succulent, bite-sized pieces of beef, lamb, chicken,

veal, or pork with a flavorful sauce, and transform

your pasta dish into a hearty, complete meal without

overloading on calories or cholesterol. Add a crisp,

colorful salad, and family and friends will leave your

table well fed and satisfied.

Rigatoni al Ragù di Vitello
(RIGATONI WITH A VEAL RAGU)

is a fairly mild meat, but stewed with the many ingredients in this recipe, it becomes a tender, rful, hearty meal.

es 4 to 6 servings

3 tbsp	**ITALPASTA olive oil**	**45 mL**
1	**medium onion, finely chopped**	**1**
3	**cloves garlic, finely chopped**	**3**
½ cup	**celery, finely chopped**	**125 mL**
½ cup	**carrots, finely chopped**	**125 mL**
¼ lb	**pancetta, finely diced**	**125 g**
2 cups	**mushrooms, quartered**	**500 mL**
1 lb	**veal shoulder, minced**	**500 g**
pinch	**salt**	**pinch**
pinch	**pepper**	**pinch**
½ cup	**dry white wine**	**125 mL**
1	**ITALPASTA 28-oz (796 mL) tin plum tomatoes, finely chopped with their juice**	**1**
2 tbsp	**fresh basil, chopped**	**25 mL**
1 tsp	**dried oregano**	**5 mL**
1 lb	**ITALPASTA Rigatoni**	**500 g**
¼ cup	**pecorino or Parmesan cheese, freshly grated**	**50 mL**

Heat the olive oil in a large saucepan and sauté the onion, garlic, celery, and carrots until the onion is translucent. Add the pancetta and mushrooms, and continue to sauté until the pancetta is lightly browned.

Add the minced veal, salt, and pepper and sauté over medium heat until the meat begins to brown and the excess liquid has evaporated.

Add the wine, tomatoes, basil, and oregano. Bring the sauce to a boil, stirring frequently. Reduce the heat and let simmer for about 30 minutes. If the sauce becomes too thick, more wine can be added.

While the sauce is simmering, cook the pasta *al dente* in a large pot of boiling, lightly salted water. Drain, and when the sauce is ready, add the pasta, toss or stir well, and serve with the freshly grated cheese.

Radiatori con Fegato di Pollo e Asparagi
(RADIATOR PASTA WITH CHICKEN LIVER AND ASPARAGUS)

Of the many innards (heart, sweetbreads, etc.), chicken liver is my favorite — although sweetbreads rank a close second. Its unique flavor and tenderness inspired this recipe, prepared with asparagus (my favorite vegetable).

Makes 4 to 6 servings

2 tbsp	**ITALPASTA olive oil**	**25 mL**
¼ lb	**pancetta, diced**	**125 g**
1½ lb	**chicken liver, cut into quarters**	**750 g**
3	**cloves garlic, finely chopped**	**3**
2 cups	**mushrooms, sliced**	**500 mL**
1 lb	**asparagus (thicker pieces, woody stems removed), cut diagonally into 1-inch (2.5 cm) pieces, keeping the flower whole**	**500 g**
1	**large sweet red pepper, cut into ¼-inch (5 mm) by 1½-inch (4 cm) pieces**	**1**
3 tbsp	**fresh oregano, finely chopped**	**45 mL**
3 tbsp	**fresh rosemary, finely chopped**	**45 mL**
½ tsp	**chili peppers, crushed**	**2 mL**
4	**large ripe tomatoes, peeled, seeded, and diced into ¼-inch (5 mm) pieces**	**4**
1 cup	**whipping cream**	**250 mL**
1 tbsp	**butter**	**15 mL**
¼ tsp	**nutmeg**	**1 mL**
¼ tsp	**pepper**	**1 mL**
½ cup	**Parmesan cheese, freshly grated**	**125 mL**
1 lb	**ITALPASTA Plain or Vegetable Radiators**	**500 g**
3 tbsp	**fresh parsley, chopped**	**45 mL**

1. Bring a large pot of lightly salted water to a boil.
2. In a large skillet or saucepan, heat the oil and add the pancetta and chicken livers. Sauté over medium heat until they begin to brown.
3. Add the garlic, mushrooms, asparagus, red peppers, oregano, rosemary, and chili peppers. Toss or stir well and continue to sauté over medium-high heat for about 2 minutes or until the mushrooms begin to soften. Do not burn the garlic.
4. Add the diced tomatoes, toss or stir, then add cream, butter, nutmeg, pepper, and Parmesan cheese. Reduce the heat and cook until the sauce has thickened.
5. When the water has come to a boil, add the pasta and cook *al dente*, then drain well in a colander. Add pasta to the sauce along with the fresh parsley. Toss and serve, covering with any remaining sauce.

Radiatori con Vitello, Marsala e Funghi

(RADIATOR PASTA WITH VEAL AND MUSHROOMS IN A MARSALA WINE SAUCE)

When I think of using Marsala wine in a recipe, I think of how sweet life is that we have this wonderful drink to enhance our foods. In this dish, the Marsala creates a uniquely flavored sauce and there should only be enough to coat the pasta.

Makes 4 to 6 servings

1½ lb	leg of veal, cut into ½-inch (1 cm) thick slices and pounded flat (scallopini) (can be prepared by a butcher)	750 g
2 tbsp	ITALPASTA olive oil	25 mL
pinch	salt	pinch
pinch	black pepper, freshly ground	pinch
2 tbsp	butter	25 mL
2 cups	mushrooms, sliced	500 mL
1 cup	Marsala wine	250 mL
½ cup	dry white wine	125 mL
¼ cup	chicken stock (page 123)	50 mL
1	sweet red pepper, julienne*	1
1 lb	ITALPASTA Plain or Vegetable Radiators	500 g
¼ cup	fresh parsley, finely chopped	50 mL

Julienne is strips 2 inches (5 cm) long by ¼ inch (5 mm) wide

1. Cut the veal cutlets into 1½-inch (4 cm) by ¼-inch (5 mm) strips.
2. In a large skillet, heat the olive oil and, over medium-high heat, add the veal, salt, and pepper and sauté the veal until it begins to brown. Remove the excess oil and add butter and mushrooms. Reduce the heat to medium and continue to sauté until the mushrooms begin to soften, about 2 minutes.
3. Add the Marsala wine. (The heat of the pan will cause it to sizzle.) Then add the white wine, chicken stock, and red peppers and simmer until it is reduced by half, about 5 minutes. Remove from heat while you prepare the pasta.
4. Bring a large pot of lightly salted water to a boil and add the pasta. Cook the pasta *al dente*, stirring constantly so that it does not stick together. Drain the pasta, and bring the sauce to a boil. Add the pasta to the sauce, toss or stir well, and serve sprinkled with parsley.

Rotini alla Finanziere

(ROTINI WITH CHICKEN LIVERS AND PIMENTO OLIVES)

This dish comes from a chef who had just left his homeland of Italy. He told me that it meant "the farmer's wife would cook what she brought back from the fields that day." Since I do not go to the fields, this is my version.

Makes 4 to 6 servings

2 tbsp	ITALPASTA olive oil	25 mL
1	small onion, diced	1
2	cloves garlic, chopped	2
2 cups	mushrooms, sliced	500 mL
1½ lb	chicken liver, cut into quarters	750 g
½ cup	prosciutto, diced	125 mL
½ cup	pimento olives, sliced	125 mL
3	plum tomatoes, peeled, seeded, and diced	3
1 tbsp	ITALPASTA tomato paste	15 mL
6 oz	beef stock (page 120)	175 mL
½ cup	dry red wine	125 mL
1	small red pepper, diced	1
1 tsp	basil	5 mL
1 tsp	nutmeg	5 mL
pinch	salt	pinch
pinch	pepper	pinch
1 lb	ITALPASTA Rotini	500 g

1. Bring a pot of lightly salted water to boil.
2. Heat oil in a large pan. Sauté the onion, garlic, mushrooms, liver, and prosciutto for 3 to 5 minutes or until the liver begins to brown.
3. Add the remaining ingredients, stir well, and simmer for 15 to 20 minutes, or until the sauce thickens.
4. Meanwhile, add the pasta to the boiling water, cook *al dente* and drain well.
5. Add the pasta to the sauce and simmer for 1 minute. Spoon the pasta on dinner plates or a large serving dish, spoon the sauce over top, and serve immediately.

Bocconcini con Pollo e Formaggi

(BOCCONCINI WITH CHICKEN, SUN-DRIED TOMATOES AND CHEESES)

For the cheese lover, this dish offers a strong but memorable taste. Take care with this recipe, remembering that the cheeses are all slightly salty.

Makes 4 to 6 servings

2 tbsp	butter	25 mL
2 tbsp	ITALPASTA extra virgin olive oil	25 mL
1½ lb	boneless chicken breast, cut into ¼-inch (5 mm) strips	750 g
2 cups	oyster mushrooms, coarsely cut	500 mL
5	sprigs fresh rosemary, chopped	5
4	cloves garlic, finely chopped	4
½ cup	sun-dried tomatoes, thinly sliced	125 mL
¼ tsp	black pepper, freshly ground	1 mL
1 cup	dry white wine	250 mL
⅓ cup	Parmesan cheese, freshly grated	75 mL
⅓ cup	Romano cheese, freshly grated	75 mL
⅓ cup	Asiago cheese, freshly grated	75 mL
1 lb	ITALPASTA Bocconcini	500 g
¼ cup	fresh parsley, chopped	50 mL

1. Bring a pot of lightly salted water to a boil.
2. Heat the butter and oil in a large skillet. Add the chicken and sauté over medium-high heat until the meat is brown. Add the mushrooms, rosemary, garlic, dried tomatoes, and pepper. Continue to sauté until the garlic is clear and the tomatoes and mushrooms begin to soften.
3. Reduce the heat and add the white wine. Let simmer until mixture is reduced by half. Add half of each of the three cheeses and toss or stir well. Remove from heat.
4. When the water comes to a boil, cook the pasta *al dente*. Return the chicken to the stove, drain the pasta, add to the pan, and toss or stir with the parsley and the remaining cheeses. Heat through (about 1 minute) and serve.

Vermicelli con Pollo al Limone

(VERMICELLI WITH CHICKEN IN A CREAMY LEMON SAUCE)

A delicate flavor of cream, lemon, and brandy makes this recipe a simple yet exciting meal to prepare and enjoy.

Makes 4 to 6 servings

3 tbsp	butter	45 mL
1	medium onion, diced	1
1½ cups	mushrooms, sliced	375 mL
1½ lb	chicken breast, cut into thin strips	750 g
¼ cup	flour	50 mL
3 tbsp	brandy	45 mL
½ cup	dry white wine	125 mL
1 tbsp	lemon juice	15 mL
1 tbsp	lemon zest	15 mL
1 cup	whipping cream	250 mL
¼ cup	Parmesan cheese, freshly grated	50 mL
pinch	white pepper	pinch
pinch	nutmeg	pinch
1 lb	ITALPASTA Vermicelli	500 g
6	lemon slices, twisted for garnish	6
4	sprigs parsley for garnish	4

1. Bring a large pot of lightly salted water to a boil.
2. In a large skillet, heat the butter and sauté the onions and mushrooms until softened.
3. Dust the chicken in flour and add to the skillet. Continue to sauté until brown, stirring frequently. Add the brandy and white wine and reduce liquid by half. Add half the lemon juice, all the lemon zest and toss or stir well.
4. Add the whipping cream, Parmesan cheese, white pepper, and nutmeg. With a whisk, stir the sauce until smooth. Simmer for 2 to 3 minutes until the sauce begins to thicken and the chicken is cooked.
5. Check the sauce for tartness and, if necessary, add more lemon juice. The sauce should have just a hint of lemon flavoring.
6. Cook the pasta *al dente*, drain well, and add to the sauce. Toss or stir well. Put the pasta on a serving dish or individual plates and spoon the chicken and sauce over the pasta. Garnish with lemon slices and sprigs of parsley.

apellini d' Angelo con Scaloppine e Salsa di Funghi

(SAUTÉED SCALLOPINI WITH WILD MUSHROOM CREAM SAUCE AND ANGEL HAIR PASTA)

There is nothing like the flavor of mushrooms simmering in a cream sauce with sautéed veal. Serve with pasta and enjoy a meal to remember.

Makes 4 servings

2 tbsp	**ITALPASTA olive oil, divided**	25 mL
2 tbsp	**butter, divided**	25 mL
¾ lb	**wild mushrooms, such as chanterelles, shiitake, oyster, or a combination, sliced in half (leave whole if they are small)**	375 g
½ cup	**shallots, finely chopped**	125 mL
2	**cloves garlic, finely chopped**	2
1 tbsp	**fresh thyme, finely chopped**	15 mL
pinch	**salt**	pinch
pinch	**pepper**	pinch
½ cup	**dry white wine**	125 mL
1 cup	**beef stock (page 122)**	250 mL
1½ lb	**veal scallopini, cut into 2-oz (60 g) fillets, flattened with a mallet and cut into 3-inch (8 cm) by ½-inch (1 cm) strips**	750 g
¼ tsp	**salt**	1 mL
pinch	**pepper**	pinch
¼ cup	**flour**	50 mL
1 cup	**whipping cream**	250 mL
1 tsp	**fresh chervil, minced**	5 mL
1 tsp	**fresh lemon juice**	5 mL
8	**large sweet strawberries, sliced about ¼-inch (5 mm) thick for garnish**	8
1 lb	**ITALPASTA Angel Hair (Capellini) parsley flowers for garnish**	500 g

1. Bring a large pot of lightly salted water to a boil.
2. Meanwhile, heat 1 tsp (5 mL) of oil and 1 tsp (5 mL) of butter in a large skillet or saucepan. Add the mushrooms and sauté 3 to 5 minutes or until they soften.
3. Add the shallots, garlic, thyme, salt, and pepper and continue to sauté for 2 minutes. Add the wine and reduce liquid by half. Add the beef stock and simmer for 5 minutes or until the liquid is reduced.
4. While this is simmering, in another skillet heat 1 tbsp (15 mL) of olive oil and 1 tbsp (15 mL) of butter. Season the veal strips with salt and pepper, dust in flour and shake off the excess. Brown the meat on both sides and, using a pair of tongs, add to the simmering sauce. Discard the frying oil.
5. Add the cream and continue to heat until the veal is cooked through and the sauce has thickened slightly, adding the chervil and lemon juice.
6. While this is simmering, cook the pasta in the boiling water *al dente*. Drain well and add to the sauce. Toss or stir well. Using tongs, remove the pasta from the pan and place on a large serving dish or individual plates. Spoon the sauce over the pasta making sure the veal is evenly distributed. Garnish with the sliced strawberries and parsley flowers.

Capelli d'Angelo con Pollo e Funghi

(ANGEL HAIR PASTA WITH CHICKEN, WILD MUSHROOMS, AND HERBS)

Although there is a mixture of fresh herbs in this aromatic dish, it is the watercress that stands out and adds a gentle flavor. The less you cook the basil and watercress, the more flavor they'll give.

Makes 4 to 6 servings

2 tbsp	ITALPASTA olive oil	25 mL
1½ lb	chicken breast, cut into 2-inch (5 cm) strips	750 g
pinch	salt	pinch
pinch	pepper	pinch
3 tbsp	butter	45 mL
1 cup	wild mushrooms, sliced	250 mL
4	shallots, finely chopped	4
½ cup	dry white wine	125 mL
1 cup	chicken stock (page 123)	250 mL
3	plum tomatoes, peeled, seeded, and diced	3
2 tbsp	fresh basil, chopped	25 mL
2 tbsp	fresh oregano, chopped	25 mL
2 cups	watercress, with stems	500 mL
1 lb	ITALPASTA Angel Hair (Capellini)	500 g
¼ cup	Parmesan cheese, freshly grated additional Parmesan cheese	50 mL

1. Bring a pot of lightly salted water to a boil.
2. Meanwhile, in a medium saucepan or skillet, heat olive oil. Season the chicken with salt and pepper and sauté in oil until browned on all sides but not fully cooked. Remove from the pan with a slotted spoon and place on a paper towel to absorb any excess oil.
3. Remove the remaining oil from the pan and add the butter and mushrooms. Sauté until mushrooms begin to soften. Add shallots and continue cooking until they begin to sizzle (take care not to burn them). Add the wine to the pan and then the chicken stock. Allow this liquid to thicken, about 5 minutes.
4. Add the browned chicken, diced tomatoes, basil, oregano, and watercress. Mix well and allow this to simmer until the chicken is cooked. This should not take longer than 5 minutes. (You want to retain the redness and firmness of the tomatoes and the bright green of the watercress.) The watercress should be just wilted. Adjust the salt and pepper if necessary.
5. While this is simmering, add the pasta to the boiling water and cook *al dente*. Drain well and add to the chicken and mushrooms. Toss or stir well with the Parmesan cheese and serve sprinkled with additional Parmesan cheese.

Pennine Lisce con Saltimbocca alla Marsala

(PENNE WITH VEAL AND PROSCIUTTO IN A MARSALA WINE SAUCE)

The term "Saltimbocca" literally means to jump in your mouth. The flavors will bombard you.

Makes 4 to 6 servings

1½ lb	veal scallopini cut into 4-oz (125 g) cutlets and pounded flat with a meat hammer (can be prepared by butcher)	750 g
pinch	salt	pinch
pinch	black pepper, freshly ground	pinch
3 tbsp	sage (to be rubbed on veal)	45 mL
¼ lb	prosciutto ham, thinly sliced	125 g
3 tbsp	ITALPASTA olive oil	45 mL
¼ cup	flour	50 mL
3 tbsp	butter	45 mL
2 cups	oyster mushrooms, sliced	500 mL
1 cup	sweet Marsala wine	250 mL
½ cup	dry white wine	125 mL
1 lb	ITALPASTA Penne Lisce	500 g
3 tbsp	fresh parsley, chopped	45 mL
1 cup	fresh strawberries, sliced (with a squeeze of lemon juice) for garnish	250 mL

1. Lay the flattened veal out on a table or cutting board. Season with salt and pepper and rub about 2 or 3 pinches of sage on each cutlet. Lay the slices of prosciutto on top of the veal one layer thick and pat down with your finger. Using a sharp knife, cut the veal and prosciutto into ½-inch (1 cm) by 2- or 3-inch (5 or 8 cm) strips.
2. Bring a pot of lightly salted water to a boil.
3. Heat the olive oil in a large skillet. Dust the veal pieces in the flour, shake off the excess and place in the hot olive oil over medium-high heat, prosciutto side down. Allow veal to turn a rich golden-brown and, with a pair of tongs, turn the veal over and sauté for about 30 seconds. Remove from heat and set aside. Carefully pour off the excess oil from the pan.
4. Return the pan to the stove and add the butter. Over medium heat allow the butter to melt, then add the mushrooms. Continue to sauté until the mushrooms begin to soften, then add the Marsala and white wines. Reduce heat to medium or medium-low and let the sauce simmer until it thickens. This sauce should reach the consistency of a glaze and there should be only enough to completely coat the pasta.
5. Cook the pasta *al dente*. Drain well in a colander and add to the wine sauce. Toss well and serve sprinkled generously with parsley and garnished with fresh strawberry slices. Do not worry if some of the prosciutto separates from the veal.

Agnello al Forno con Spaghetti All'Aglio

(ROAST RACK OF LAMB WITH GARLIC SPAGHETTI)

Though the rack is the most expensive cut of the lamb, I have always found it to be the most tender and flavorful. I love it with Dijon mustard and roasted garlic. Add an extra helping of garlic spaghetti and a little of red wine and I'm in heaven.

Makes 2 to 4 servings

Lamb

1	**rack of lamb (8 chops) with chime bone removed (your butcher will do this)**	1
1 tbsp	**Dijon mustard**	15 mL
1 tbsp	**garlic, finely chopped**	15 mL
1 tsp	**rosemary**	5 mL
1 tsp	**thyme**	5 mL
pinch	**black pepper, freshly ground**	pinch

Pasta

½ lb	**ITALPASTA Fettuccine**	250 g
3 tbsp	**butter**	45 mL
1 tbsp	**ITALPASTA extra virgin olive oil**	15 mL
5	**cloves garlic, finely chopped**	5
pinch	**black pepper, freshly ground**	pinch
½ cup	**Parmesan cheese, freshly grated**	125 mL
3 tbsp	**fresh parsley, chopped**	45 mL
¼ cup	**additional Parmesan cheese**	50 mL
	halved cherry tomatoes for garnish	
	parsley flowers for garnish	

1. Preheat the oven to 375°F (190°C).
2. Bring a pot of lightly salted water to a boil.
3. To prepare the lamb, first remove any excess fat from the top of the rack (this can be done by pulling it off with your fingers or using a sharp boning knife).
4. Using a sharp boning knife, clear the fat from the end of the chop going up the bone about 1 inch (2.5 cm) so that the ends of the 7 or 8 bones of the rack are exposed. Then make diagonal cuts on the meat of the rack no deeper than ¼ inch (5 mm).
5. Make a mixture of the Dijon mustard, garlic, rosemary, thyme, and pepper. Generously cover the entire top of the rack and place it in the oven for 3 to 5 minutes. This will roast the lamb to medium rare. If you prefer, it only takes another 5 minutes to bring it to well done.
6. When the water is boiling, cook the pasta *al dente* and drain.
7. In a large skillet, heat the butter and oil and sauté the garlic. Add the drained pasta, freshly ground black pepper, and Parmesan cheese. Toss or stir well so that the pasta is well coated with the butter and garlic and transfer to a serving dish or individual plates.
8. When the lamb is done, cut it vertically so that you will have 6 or 8 chops, being careful not to loosen the glazed baked mustard. Arrange the chops around the pasta. Sprinkle with additional Parmesan cheese and garnish with cherry tomatoes and parsley flowers.

Agnello al Forno con Frutta Sciroppata di Pomodoro e Mango

(ROASTED RACK OF LAMB WITH TOMATO AND MANGO COMPOTE)

A bit of work to prepare this dish, but the lamb deserves it and so do you. I truthfully cannot remember what inspired the mango sauce, but it seems that it was meant to be.

Makes 4 servings

1 lb	**ITALPASTA Bucatini**	**500 g**
1	**rack of lamb (8 chops) with chime bone**	**1**
	removed (your butcher will do this)	
	parsley flowers for garnish	

Lamb Marinade

4	**cloves garlic, finely chopped**	**4**
2 tbsp	**fresh rosemary**	**25 mL**
1 tbsp	**fresh thyme**	**15 mL**
1 tbsp	**fresh oregano**	**15 mL**
¼ cup	**ITALPASTA extra virgin olive oil**	**50 mL**
pinch	**salt**	**pinch**
pinch	**black pepper, freshly ground**	**pinch**

Mango Compote

2 tbsp	**butter**	**25 mL**
½ cup	**onion, diced**	**125 mL**
2 tbsp	**garlic, finely minced**	**25 mL**
¼ cup	**carrots, diced**	**50 mL**
¼ cup	**celery, diced**	**50 mL**
½ cup	**dry red wine**	**125 mL**
3 cups	**plum tomatoes, peeled, seeded, and diced**	**750 mL**
1	**large mango, peeled, pit removed (half diced**	**1**
	for the sauce and remaining sliced for garnish)	
¼ cup	**black olives, chopped**	**50 mL**
2 tbsp	**ITALPASTA anchovies, very finely chopped**	**25 mL**

1. Add the garlic, rosemary, thyme, and oregano to the olive oil.
2. Using a sharp knife, make diagonal cuts on the top of the rack one way, the the other about ⅛-inch (3 mm) deep and an inch apart. Marinate the lamb in the oil mixture, season with salt and black pepper, and let stand overnight in the refrigerator.
3. Roast at 400°F (200°C) for 35 minutes until medium rare or longer as desired. It will take only 5 more minutes to reach well done so be careful of your time.
4. Bring a pot of lightly salted water to a boil.
5. For the Mango Compote: In a large saucepan or skillet heat the butter and add the onions, garlic, carrots, and celery and sauté. Be careful not to burn the garlic or onions.
6. Add the red wine and reduce by half. Add the tomatoes, diced mango, olive and anchovies and, over medium heat, cook until most of the juice from the tomatoes has evaporated and the sauce is reduced.
7. Meanwhile, add the pasta to the boiling water and cook *al dente*. Drain and toss with the sauce.
8. Using tongs, put the pasta on a large serving dish or individual plates and spoon the leftover sauce on top. Carve the lamb into chops and arrange on the plate or platter. Garnish with the sliced mango and parsley flowers.

Penne con Pollo Picatto
(PENNE WITH CHICKEN IN A LEMON SAUCE)

...tto is a traditional style incorporating quick cooking with lemon, butter, and white wine. Here is a ...sion with penne and chicken breasts.

...kes 2 to 4 servings

2 tbsp	butter	25 mL
1 tbsp	ITALPASTA olive oil	15 mL
1½ lb	chicken breast, julienne*	750 g
¼ cup	flour	50 mL
½ cup	dry white wine	125 mL
1 cup	chicken stock (page 123)	250 mL
2 tbsp	lemon juice	25 mL
½ tsp	lemon zest	2 mL
1	large sweet red pepper, julienne	1
2 tbsp	fresh chives, chopped	25 mL
2 tbsp	fresh parsley, chopped	25 mL
pinch	salt	pinch
pinch	pepper	pinch
½ lb	ITALPASTA Penne	250 g

*Julienne is strips 2 inches (5 cm) long by ¼ inch (5 mm) wide

In a large skillet or frying pan, heat the butter and oil. Season the chicken pieces and dust with the flour. Shake off the excess and sauté the chicken in the butter and oil until brown but still raw in the center.

Add the white wine, chicken stock, lemon juice, lemon zest, and red peppers and continue to cook until the sauce is reduced slightly and the chicken is cooked. Remove from heat.

Add the chives and parsley, and season with salt and pepper.

Bring a pot of lightly salted water to a boil, cook the pasta *al dente*, and drain. Return to the heat and add the pasta to the lemon sauce, toss or stir a few times, and place on a large serving dish. Serve immediately.

Penne Rigate al Coniglio
(PENNE RIGATE WITH RABBIT AND JUNIPER)

If you dare to venture, this stewed rabbit with juniper and herbs will leave you very satisfied. To my surprise, it is popular in our North American culture.

Makes 4 to 6 servings

2 tbsp	butter	25 mL
2 tbsp	ITALPASTA extra virgin olive oil	25 mL
½ cup	onion, finely diced	125 mL
3	cloves garlic, finely chopped	3
½ cup	carrots, finely diced	125 mL
½ cup	celery, finely diced	125 mL
1½ lb	boneless rabbit cut into ½-inch (1 cm) cubes or strips	750 g
¼ cup	juniper berries	50 mL
1 tbsp	fresh rosemary, finely chopped	15 mL
1 tbsp	fresh thyme, finely chopped	15 mL
1½ cups	dry red wine	375 mL
2 cups	ITALPASTA tinned plum tomatoes with juice, coarsely chopped	500 mL
¼ cup	chicken stock (page 123)	50 mL
pinch	salt	pinch
pinch	black pepper, freshly ground	pinch
1 lb	ITALPASTA Penne Rigate	500 g
¾ cup	Parmesan cheese, freshly grated	175 mL

1. In a large skillet or deep frying pan, heat the butter and oil over medium heat and sauté the onion until golden. Add the garlic, carrots, and celery and continue to sauté until the carrots begin to brown, about 3 to 5 minutes. Take care not to burn the garlic.
2. Add the rabbit, juniper berries, rosemary, and thyme. Continue to cook until the meat begins to brown, stirring frequently.
3. Increase the heat and add the red wine. The heat should cause it to bubble and reduce immediately. Add the tomatoes, chicken stock, salt, and pepper and bring to a boil. Reduce the heat and let simmer for about 20 minutes or until the rabbit is tender.
4. Bring a large pot of lightly salted water to a boil and add the pasta. Stir well so that the pasta does not stick. When the pasta is cooked *al dente*, drain and add to the sauce. Add the Parmesan cheese, toss well, and serve at once.

Penne al Ragù di Agnello

(PENNE WITH LAMB RAGU)

Ragù generally refers to meats and vegetables stewed together, for blending flavors.

Makes 4 servings

1 cup	dried porcine mushrooms	250 mL
2 tbsp	ITALPASTA olive oil	25 mL
2 tbsp	butter	25 mL
1	medium yellow onion, finely diced	1
½ cup	peeled carrots, finely diced	125 mL
½ cup	celery, finely diced	125 mL
1 lb	boneless lamb shoulder, cut into ½-inch (1 cm) to 1-inch (2.5 cm) cubes	500 g
2 tbsp	fresh rosemary, finely chopped (or 1 tsp/5 mL dried)	25 mL
½ cup	dry white wine	125 mL
1	ITALPASTA 28-oz (796 mL) tin plum tomatoes, finely chopped	1
1 lb	ITALPASTA Penne	500 g
¼ cup	Parmesan cheese, freshly grated	50 mL
2 tbsp	fresh parsley, finely chopped	25 mL
pinch	salt	pinch
pinch	pepper	pinch

Soak the mushrooms in 1 cup (250 mL) of lukewarm water for about 20 minutes. Lift them out, squeeze the excess water back into the bowl and chop them finely. Filter the water through a paper towel or coffee filter and set aside. Put the olive oil and butter in a sauce pan and, over medium-low heat, sauté the onion, carrots, and celery until the onion is golden and the vegetables are lightly browned.

Raise the heat to medium-high. Add the lamb and rosemary and continue to sauté until the meat begins to brown, stirring frequently.

Add the wine, mushrooms, filtered water, and tomatoes with their juice. Once the sauce has come to a boil, reduce the heat and continue to simmer for about 5 minutes. Remove from heat and set aside.

In a large pot of boiling, lightly salted water, cook the pasta *al dente* and drain. Return the sauce to medium heat, add the pasta to the sauce, and toss or stir well. Serve at once, sprinkled with grated Parmesan cheese, salt, pepper, and parsley.

Penne all'Italiana

(PENNE WITH A PORK TENDERLOIN IN A SAUCE)

The use of the cured meats adds a regional flavor to this dish. A different taste with every mouthful.

Makes 4 servings

½ lb	ITALPASTA Penne	250 g
2 tbsp	ITALPASTA olive oil	25 mL
2 tbsp	butter	25 mL
1	onion, diced	1
3	cloves garlic, finely chopped	3
½ lb	pork tenderloin, cut into ½-inch (1 cm) cubes	250 g
¼ lb	chicken livers, sliced	125 g
6 tbsp	prosciutto, diced into ¼-inch (5 mm) pieces	90 mL
6 tbsp	spicy capicolla, diced into ¼-inch (5 mm) pieces	90 mL
¼ cup	bacon or pancetta, chopped	50 mL
½ cup	red wine	125 mL
4	plum tomatoes, peeled and diced	4
1	sweet red pepper, coarsely diced	1
½ cup	beef stock (page 120)	125 mL
2 tsp	ITALPASTA tomato paste	10 mL
1 tsp	basil	5 mL
1 tsp	rosemary	5 mL
pinch	nutmeg	pinch
pinch	salt	pinch
¼ tsp	pepper	1 mL
2 tbsp	Parmesan cheese, freshly grated additional Parmesan cheese	25 mL

1. Bring a large pot of lightly salted water to a boil. Cook pasta *al dente* and drain.
2. In a large skillet heat the oil and butter, add the onion, garlic, pork tenderloin, chicken livers, prosciutto, capicolla, and pancetta and sauté for about 5 minutes or until brown.
3. Add the red wine and reduce slightly. Add the diced tomatoes, stir well, and add all remaining ingredients except the Parmesan. Let simmer for about 15 minutes or until the sauce begins to thicken. Add 2 tbsp (25 mL) of Parmesan cheese, and stir well. (This will help give body to the sauce and add flavor.)
4. Add the cooked pasta to the sauce and toss or stir well.
5. Serve on a platter or individual plates sprinkled with additional Parmesan cheese.

ʒg Noodles alla Bolognese

ʒ NOODLES WITH A BOLOGNESE SAUCE)

̄e is nothing like a hearty meat sauce drenched over your favorite pasta to warm you on those cold
̄er days. A simple dish, but one with so much heart.

̄es 4 to 6 servings

1 lb	ITALPASTA medium or broad Egg Noodles	500 g
5 cups	Salsa alla Bolognese (page 122)	1.25 L
	Parmesan cheese, freshly grated	

Bring a large pot of lightly salted water to a boil and cook pasta *al dente*.
Reheat or prepare fresh Bolognese sauce.
When the pasta is cooked and drained you have two choices:

A. Add the pasta to the sauce. Toss or stir well and, using a pair of tongs,
put the pasta on a serving dish or individual plates and ladle the remaining
sauce over top. Sprinkle with Parmesan cheese and serve.

OR

B. Place the pasta on a serving dish or individual plates and ladle the sauce
over top. Sprinkle with Parmesan cheese and serve.

Fusilli alla "Ruffo"

(TRI-COLORED FUSILLI WITH CHICKEN AND HERBS)

This dish is named after the owner of Ruffo's, an Italian restaurant. Ruffo's mother taught me to make it,
and I'm glad she did.

Makes 4 to 6 servings

3 tbsp	ITALPASTA extra virgin olive oil	45 mL
1½ lb	boneless chicken breast, cut into thin strips	750 g
½ cup	pancetta or bacon diced into ¼-inch (5 mm) pieces	125 mL
4	cloves garlic, finely chopped	4
1	medium leek, white part only, thinly sliced	1
5 tbsp	fresh basil, finely chopped	70 mL
2 tbsp	fresh oregano, finely chopped	25 mL
½ cup	dry white wine	125 mL
1	ITALPASTA 28-oz (796 mL) tin plum tomatoes, finely chopped	1
pinch	salt	pinch
pinch	black pepper, freshly ground	pinch
1 lb	ITALPASTA Tri-Colored Fusilli	500 g
½ cup	ricotta cheese	125 mL
2 tbsp	chopped fresh parsley	25 mL

1. Bring a pot of lightly salted water to a boil.
2. Meanwhile, heat the oil in a large skillet over medium-high heat. Season the
chicken with salt and pepper. Sauté the chicken and the bacon until the
chicken is browned on all sides and the bacon is crispy. Reduce the heat to
medium and add the garlic, leeks, basil, and oregano and continue to sauté,
tossing or stirring often, until the garlic begins to change color.
3. Add the wine and let simmer until the liquid is reduced by half. Add the
tomatoes, salt, and pepper. Stir well and let simmer for about 3 to 5 minutes
or until the sauce has thickened. Remove from the heat and set aside.
4. When the water comes to a boil, add the pasta and cook *al dente*. Drain well
in a colander or strainer. Break the cheese into little pieces and stir into the
sauce. Add the pasta, toss or stir well, and serve immediately.

Gnocchi alle Boscaiuolo

(GNOCCHI PASTA WITH ITALIAN SAUSAGE AND MUSHROOM)

The cream in this dish captures the flavor of the sausage, and this flavor is then bound to the pasta. You can replace the cream with diced plum tomatoes or use a combination of the two. Try this for a special lunch.

Makes 4 to 6 servings

1½ lb	Italian sausage, spicy or sweet	750 g
2 tbsp	ITALPASTA olive oil	25 mL
1	large sweet red pepper, diced	1
2 cups	mushrooms, sliced	500 mL
1 cup	dry white wine	250 mL
2 cups	whipping cream	500 mL
¼ cup	Parmesan cheese, freshly grated	50 mL
½ tsp	nutmeg	2 mL
pinch	salt	pinch
pinch	black pepper, freshly ground	pinch
pinch	chili pepper, crushed	pinch
1 cup	frozen peas	250 mL
1 lb	ITALPASTA Gnocchi	500 g

1. In a medium-sized pot, boil the sausages so they are slightly cooked and pink on the inside. Rinse in cold water then cut into thin slices.
2. Bring a pot of lightly salted water to a boil.
3. In a large skillet, heat the oil and sauté the sausage slices, red peppers, and mushrooms until the sausages turn a golden color. Add the wine and let this thicken.
4. Add the cream, Parmesan, nutmeg, salt, pepper, and chili pepper and simmer until mixture has thickened. Add the peas and simmer for 1 more minute so that the peas are heated through. Remove from the heat and set aside.
5. When the water comes to a boil, add the pasta and cook *al dente*. Return the sauce to the stove, drain the pasta and add it to the sauce. Toss well and serve.

Linguine con Salsiccia e Panna

(LINGUINE WITH SAUSAGES, TOMATOES, AND CREAM)

The term "panna" refers to this recipe being prepared in a pan with cream.

Makes 4 to 6 servings

1 lb	Italian pork sausages, mild or spicy	500 g
2 tbsp	butter	25 mL
1 tbsp	ITALPASTA olive oil	15 mL
2 tsp	fresh rosemary, finely chopped (or 1 tsp/5 mL dried)	10 mL
6	fresh plum tomatoes, seeded, and finely diced	6
¼ tsp	salt	1 mL
¼ tsp	pepper	1 mL
pinch	red pepper flakes	pinch
½ cup	dry white wine	125 mL
1 lb	ITALPASTA Linguine	500 g
1 cup	whipping cream	250 mL
2 tbsp	parsley, finely chopped	25 mL
¼ cup	Parmesan, freshly grated	50 mL

1. Boil the sausage in water for 2 to 3 minutes. Cool in cold water, drain, then slice them into rounds about ¼-inch (5 mm) thick.
2. Melt the butter and oil in a large saucepan. Add the sausage and cook until lightly browned. Add the rosemary, tomatoes, salt, pepper, red pepper flakes and wine. Cook until the wine is reduced and the tomatoes begin to form a sauce, about 5 to 7 minutes.
3. In the meantime, bring a large pot of lightly salted water to a boil, cook the pasta *al dente*, and drain.
4. Pour the cream into the pan and add the parsley. Cook, stirring frequently, until the sauce is reduced and thickened slightly.
5. Add the pasta to the sauce along with the grated cheese. Toss or stir well and serve immediately.

Fettuccine con Pollo alla Fiorentina

(FETTUCCINE WITH CHICKEN AND SPINACH)

This is one of those dishes that has a lot of ingredients. But they all combine for the greater good — a melange of fettuccine with chicken and spinach.

Makes 4 servings

1½ lb	boneless chicken breast, cut into ½-inch (1 cm) by 2-inch (5 cm) strips	750 g
2 tbsp	ITALPASTA olive oil	25 mL
3 tbsp	ITALPASTA extra virgin olive oil	45 mL
1	medium onion, diced	1
4	cloves garlic, chopped	4
2 cups	mushrooms, sliced	500 mL
3	bunches fresh spinach, washed, stems removed, and coarsely cut	3
½ cup	dry white wine	125 mL
4	large plum tomatoes, peeled, seeded, and diced	4
2 tbsp	fresh basil, chopped	25 mL
1 tsp	ITALPASTA tomato paste	5 mL
1 tsp	sugar	5 mL
1 tsp	oregano	5 mL
1 tsp	rosemary	5 mL
¼ tsp	salt	1 mL
pinch	black pepper, freshly ground	pinch
1 tsp	chili peppers, crushed (more or less, as desired)	5 mL
1 lb	ITALPASTA Spinach Fettuccine	500 g
¼ cup	Parmesan cheese, freshly grated	50 mL
	basil leaves for garnish	

1. Season the chicken strips with salt and pepper. Put the olive oil in a large skillet over medium-high heat. Brown the meat on both sides using prongs a spatula to turn.
2. Remove the chicken and place on a paper or cloth towel to absorb the exce oil. Discard the remaining oil and put the skillet back on the stove.
3. Bring a large pot of lightly salted water to a boil.
4. Pour the olive oil in the skillet and, over medium heat, sauté the onions and garlic until the onions begin to turn golden. Take care not to burn the garlic Add the mushrooms and continue to sauté. Add the spinach and, stirring often, continue to cook until the spinach begins to wilt, about 1 or 2 minute
5. Return the chicken to the pan and add the wine, tomatoes, basil, tomato paste, sugar, oregano, rosemary, chili peppers, salt and pepper. Stir well usi a wooden spoon. Increase the heat and bring to a boil. Then reduce the he and let simmer for about 5 minutes or until the excess liquid has evaporate and the chicken is cooked but still moist.
6. While this is simmering, cook the pasta *al dente*. Drain well and place on a serving dish or individual plates. Pour the sauce over it, sprinkle with Parmesan cheese, and garnish with basil. Serve with crusty garlic bread.

Fettuccine con Cotolette di Vitello

(FETTUCCINE WITH BREADED VEAL CUTLETS)

A traditional breaded veal cutlet accompanied by creamy fettuccine and garnished with sweet melon. A little bit of preparation, a little bit of cooking and a dinner to remember.

Makes 4 to 6 servings

¼ cup	vegetable oil	50 mL
8	veal cutlets, 2½ ounces (75 g) each	8
1½ cups	whipping cream	375 mL
2 tbsp	butter	25 mL
pinch	white pepper	pinch
½ tsp	nutmeg	2 mL
1 lb	ITALPASTA Fettuccine	500 g
1 cup	Parmesan cheese, freshly grated	250 mL
2 tbsp	chives, chopped	25 mL
	additional Parmesan cheese	
2 tbsp	parsley, chopped	25 mL
1	lemon, cut in half	1
1	small cantaloupe, peeled, and cut into thin strips	1

Breading

	breadcrumbs, for breading the veal	
2	eggs, slightly beaten with 3 tbsp (45 mL) milk in a shallow bowl for dipping the veal	2
pinch	salt	pinch
pinch	black pepper	pinch
¼ tsp	cayenne	1 mL

1. Bring a large pot of lightly salted water to a boil.
2. Wrap each piece of veal with plastic wrap and pound with a meat mallet un very thin. Season with salt and pepper. Breading: Combine the breadcrumbs with salt, pepper, and cayenne. Dip the veal in the egg mixture, letting any excess drip off. Place the veal in the breadcrumbs, coating each side completely.
3. In a skillet or frying pan, heat the oil and add the veal. Pan-fry for 1 to 2 minutes or until golden brown, flip over and continue frying until golden brown. Turn the oven to 180°F (80°C). Place the veal on an ovenproof platt and put in the oven to keep warm until the rest of the dish is completed.
4. In a large saucepan or skillet, add the cream, butter, white pepper, and nutmeg. Over medium-high heat, bring to a boil, stirring constantly. Let simmer until it thickens
5. Add the pasta to the boiling water and cook *al dente*. Drain and add to the sauce with the Parmesan cheese and chives. Toss or stir well.
6. Using tongs, remove the pasta from the sauce and make several nests on a large platter or individual plates. Spoon the remainder of the sauce on top o the pasta and sprinkle with additional cheese. Place a veal cutlet on top of each nest, top with a squeeze of lemon, and serve garnished with the cantaloupe.

CHAPTER FOUR

Classic Pasta Sauces

Unlike complicated, laboriously constructed French

sauces, Italian sauces are quick and easy to make —

and since they rely more on olive oil than butter, they

are easier on the hips and heart. They remain true to the

fresh taste of the main ingredients and even the cream

sauces are light and fresh. These recipes depend on the

flavor and texture of the ingredients for their character,

so use only the finest oils and cheeses you can afford and

the freshest herbs and vegetables you can find.

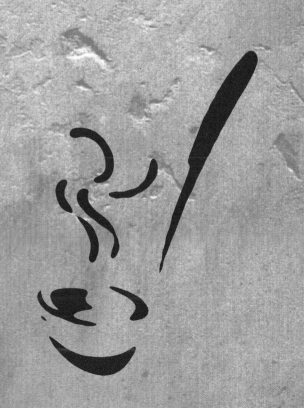

Capellini d'Angelo con Asiago, Funghi e Peperone
(CAPELLINI WITH PORTOBELLO MUSHROOMS, PEPPERS, AND ASIAGO SAUCE)

Asiago, a hard and very spicy cheese, is ideally suited for grating and adds a unique flavor to this dish. For a slight smoked flavor, grill the portobello mushrooms over an open flame and then slice them and add to the sauce while it is reducing.

Makes 4 to 6 servings

2 tbsp	ITALPASTA olive oil	25 mL
4	large portobello mushrooms, sliced	4
2 tbsp	butter	25 mL
2 tsp	garlic, finely chopped	10 mL
2 cups	whipping cream	500 mL
1 cup	Asiago cheese, grated	250 mL
pinch	salt	pinch
¼ tsp	black pepper, freshly ground	1 mL
¼ tsp	nutmeg	1 mL
1	sweet red pepper, seeded, julienne*	1
1 lb	ITALPASTA Angel Hair (Capellini)	500 g
2 oz	block of Asiago cheese, used for shavings	60 g
4 tbsp	chives, chopped	50 mL

Julienne is strips 2 inches (5 cm) long by ¼ inch (5 mm) wide

1. Bring a large pot of lightly salted water to a boil.
2. Heat the oil in a large skillet or saucepan and sauté the sliced mushrooms, turning them over with tongs so that both sides are browned. (If you choose to grill the mushrooms, exclude this step.)
3. Remove the mushrooms from the pan and place on a plate so that you can retain any juices.
4. Discard the oil in the skillet and add the butter. Add the garlic and sauté. Add the cream and grated cheese. Season with salt, pepper, and nutmeg. Bring this to a fast boil, whipping or stirring continuously with a wooden spoon so it does not burn. Add the mushrooms and its juices, reduce the heat and let simmer, whipping or stirring with a wooden spoon. When the sauce is reduced and thickened, add the red peppers and continue to heat until they are cooked but still crunchy and bright red. If you like the peppers to be more tender, simmer them in the sauce for an additional 2 to 3 minutes.
5. While the sauce is simmering with the mushrooms, add the pasta to the boiling water and cook *al dente*.
6. Drain pasta and add to the sauce. Toss or stir well. Using a pair of tongs, remove the pasta and place on a serving platter or individual plates. Pour the remaining sauce over top and place the mushrooms in a decorative manner around the pasta. Garnish with the shaved cheese and chives.

Gnocchi con Salvia e Pomodori
(GNOCCHI WITH SAGE AND TOMATOES)

Sage is an herb that doesn't receive the recognition it deserves. But add it to the smoked ricotta cheese used in this recipe (you may have to do a little searching for this), and you have the makings of some fabulous memories.

Makes 4 servings

4 tbsp	butter	50 mL
15	fresh sage leaves	15
1½	plum tomatoes, peeled, seeded, and diced	1½
¼ tsp	black pepper, freshly ground	1 mL
1 cup	whipping cream	250 mL
½ cup	Parmesan cheese, freshly grated	125 mL
¼ tsp	nutmeg	1 mL
1 lb	ITALPASTA Gnocchi	500 g
½ lb	dry ricotta cheese, smoked	250 g
	fresh parsley, chopped	

1. Bring a large pot of lightly salted water to a boil.
2. Meanwhile, add the butter to a large skillet or saucepan. Add the sage leaves and cook over medium heat until the butter is completely melted and starts to bubble.
3. Add the diced tomatoes and black pepper and simmer until the liquid has evaporated. Add the cream, Parmesan cheese, and nutmeg. Increase the heat and bring to a quick boil, then reduce the heat and simmer for 2 minutes. Stir with a wooden spoon.
4. When the water is boiling, add the pasta and cook *al dente*. Drain well, so as not to dilute the sauce. Add the pasta to the sauce and toss or stir well. Using tongs, place the pasta on a serving dish and spoon the remainder of the sauce over top. Garnish with thinly sliced dry ricotta and sprinkle with fresh chopped parsley.

Farfalle con Gorgonzola
(OW TIES WITH GORGONZOLA SAUCE)

is blue veined yet mild and creamy cheese, once only found in the Lombardy region of Italy, is now dely used throughout the world. This recipe offers a different but equally enticing version of Alfredo.

ikes 4 Servings

2 cups	whipping cream	500 mL
2 tbsp	sweet butter	25 mL
¼ tsp	white pepper	1 mL
¼ tsp	nutmeg	1 mL
pinch	salt (optional)	pinch
½ lb	Gorgonzola cheese, cut into chunks	250 g
½ lb	ITALPASTA Bow Ties	250 g
½ cup	Parmesan cheese, freshly grated	125 mL
	fresh parsley, chopped	

In a saucepan, combine the cream, butter, pepper, and nutmeg. (Salt if desired.)

Heat the cream over medium heat but do not let it boil. Stir constantly with a whisk.

Add the Gorgonzola cheese. Stir well with a whisk or a wooden spoon over low heat to melt the cheese slowly and avoid burning the cream.

Meanwhile, bring a large pot of lightly salted water to a boil and cook the pasta *al dente*. Drain and set aside until the sauce is ready.

When the sauce is smooth and glossy and all the cheese has melted, add the pasta to the sauce. Stir in well and let simmer for 2 minutes so that the pasta absorbs the subtle flavor of the sauce. Place on a serving dish or individual plates, sprinkle with the Parmesan cheese and serve immediately, topped with the parsley.

Fettuccine al Pesto di Noci
(FETTUCCINE WITH WALNUT PESTO)

So many versions of the traditional basil pesto can be created. This is one of my favorites.

Makes 4 to 6 servings

¾ lb	walnuts, shelled	375 g
1 tbsp	garlic, finely chopped	15 mL
3 tbsp	ITALPASTA extra virgin olive oil	45 mL
⅓ cup	ricotta cheese	75 mL
pinch	salt	pinch
pinch	white pepper	pinch
⅓ cup	whipping cream	75 mL
1 lb	ITALPASTA Fettuccine	500 g
⅓ cup	Parmesan cheese, freshly grated	75 mL
2 tbsp	fresh parsley, finely chopped	25 mL

1. Bring a large pot of lightly salted water to a boil.
2. Put the walnuts and garlic in a food processor and chop as finely as possible. Add the olive oil slowly and continue to process until the pureé is well blended. Add the ricotta, salt, and pepper and blend at medium speed until smooth.
3. Transfer to a large mixing bowl and whisk in the cream with a wooden spoon until smooth.
4. When the water is boiling, add the pasta and cook *al dente*. Drain well and add to the walnut sauce along with the cheese and parsley. Mix or toss well and serve immediately.

Fettuccine con Salsa di Limone
(FETTUCCINE IN A LEMON SAUCE)

A bowl of fettuccine, a creamy sauce with a hint of lemon, a glass of white wine and some crusty Italian bread. A candlelight dinner to remember. A rich but remarkably flavorful and refreshing pasta dish.

Makes 4 to 6 servings

1 cup	fresh strawberries	250 mL
⅓ cup	lemon juice, divided	75 mL
3 tbsp	butter	45 mL
2	lemons, zest only, finely chopped	2
2 cups	whipping cream	500 mL
pinch	salt	pinch
¼ tsp	white pepper	1 mL
¼ tsp	nutmeg	1 mL
1 lb	ITALPASTA Fettuccine	500 g
½ cup	Parmesan cheese, freshly grated	125 mL

1. Bring a large pot of lightly salted water to a boil.
2. Wash and slice the strawberries and place in a small mixing bowl. Add 1 tbsp (15 mL) lemon juice, toss or stir, and set aside.
3. Melt the butter in a large skillet and add ¼ cup (50 mL) lemon juice and all the zest. Cook for about half a minute. Do not let the butter burn.
4. Add the cream, salt, pepper, and nutmeg and cook the sauce, stirring frequently, until it is reduced and thickened slightly. Remove from the heat and set aside.
5. When the water is boiling, cook the pasta *al dente*. Drain well and add to the sauce.
6. Put the saucepan back on the stove, add the Parmesan cheese, toss or stir well, and cook for another 30 seconds or so. Serve garnished with the strawberries.

Fettuccine Alfredo
(FETTUCCINE ALFREDO)

A traditional dish created by the great Chef Alfredo. Here is one version of this classic recipe.

Makes 2 servings

1 cup	whipping cream*	250 mL
2 tbsp	butter	25 mL
¼ tsp	white pepper	1 mL
pinch	nutmeg	pinch
¼ cup	Parmesan cheese, freshly grated	50 mL
½ lb	ITALPASTA Fettuccine	250 g
1 tsp	parsley, freshly chopped	5 mL
	additional Parmesan cheese for serving	

1. In a large frying pan combine the whipping cream and the butter. Season with pepper and nutmeg. Cook over medium-low heat until the sauce begins to thicken, stirring frequently. Add the Parmesan a little at a time, stirring with a whisk until completely blended.
2. Meanwhile, bring a large pot of salted water to a boil and cook the pasta *al dente*. Drain the pasta well and add to the sauce. Toss or stir well and serve garnished with chopped parsley and additional Parmesan cheese if desired.

* **Increasing the cream from 1 cup (250 mL) to 1½ cups (375 mL) will make this sauce even richer.**

Mezzi Rigatoni alla Panna

(RIGATONI WITH PROSCIUTTO AND CREAM SAUCE)

...ve to cook with liquor, brandy in particular. The unique flavor of the prosciutto and the brandy give ...to this sauce, and to the pasta.

...kes 4 servings

¾ **lb**	**ITALPASTA Rigatoni**	**375 g**
2 **tbsp**	**butter**	**25 mL**
5	**green onions, finely chopped**	**5**
⅓ **lb**	**prosciutto, diced to ¼-inch (5 mm) pieces**	**170 g**
¼ **cup**	**brandy**	**60 mL**
1½ **cups**	**whipping cream**	**375 mL**
½ **cup**	**Parmesan cheese, freshly grated**	**125 mL**
pinch	**salt (optional)**	**pinch**
¼ **tsp**	**pepper**	**1 mL**
¼ **tsp**	**nutmeg**	**1 mL**
2 **tbsp**	**fresh parsley, chopped**	**25 mL**
	additional Parmesan cheese	

In a pot of lightly salted boiling water, cook the pasta *al dente*. Drain and set aside.

In a frying pan, melt the butter and sauté the onions and prosciutto over medium heat for 2 to 3 minutes.

Add the brandy, cream, cheese, salt, pepper, and nutmeg and stir well. Simmer for 2 to 3 minutes, stirring constantly until the sauce has thickened slightly.

Add the drained pasta to the sauce. Toss or stir well and serve immediately. Sprinkle with parsley and Parmesan cheese.

Spaghetti alla Carbonara

(SPAGHETTI WITH EGGS AND BACON)

This traditional dish derives its name from the generous amounts of freshly ground black peppercorn. I like to use a mix of Parmesan and Romano cheeses, although you can use the Parmesan only, as it is done in most restaurants.

Makes 4 to 6 servings

2 **tbsp**	**ITALPASTA extra virgin olive oil**	**25 mL**
2 **tbsp**	**butter**	**25 mL**
½ **lb**	**pancetta or lean bacon cut into strips**	**250 g**
	¼ inch (5 mm) thick	
½ **cup**	**dry white wine**	**125 mL**
4	**egg yolks**	**4**
2	**whole eggs**	**2**
¼ **cup**	**Parmesan cheese, freshly grated**	**50 mL**
¼ **cup**	**Romano cheese, freshly grated**	**50 mL**
3 **tbsp**	**fresh parsley, finely chopped**	**45 mL**
pinch	**salt**	**pinch**
pinch	**black peppercorn, freshly ground**	**pinch**
1 **lb**	**ITALPASTA Spaghetti**	**500 g**
	additional black peppercorn, freshly ground	

1. Bring a large pot of lightly salted water to a boil.
2. Put the oil and butter in a medium-sized skillet and, over medium-high heat, sauté the pancetta or bacon until well browned but not crisp. Add the wine and continue cooking until liquid is reduced slightly. Remove from the heat and set aside.
3. In a mixing bowl large enough to hold the pasta, lightly beat the egg yolks and whole eggs. Add the Parmesan and Romano, parsley, salt, and ground black peppercorn and lightly beat until the mixture is smooth.
4. In the boiling water, cook the pasta *al dente* and, using a colander, drain well.
5. Heat the pancetta and wine, add to the egg mixture. Add mixture to the pasta. Cook, stirring frequently, until the eggs are done.
6. Serve with a generous sprinkling of freshly ground black peppercorn.

Linguine al Pesto
(LINGUINE WITH PESTO SAUCE)

There are as many versions of pesto as there are Italian restaurants. Here is one that I have served. I know you will cherish it as much as I do.

Makes 4 to 6 servings

2 cups	fresh basil	500 mL
4	sprigs fresh parsley	4
2	sprigs fresh marjoram	2
¾ cup	pine nuts	175 g
3	cloves garlic	3
⅓ cup	Parmesan cheese, coarsely grated	75 mL
⅓ cup	Romano cheese, coarsely grated	75 mL
¼ cup	ITALPASTA olive oil	50 mL
¼ cup	chicken stock (page 123)	50 mL
1 lb	ITALPASTA Linguine	500 g
15	fresh basil leaves, for garnish	15
½ cup	additional Parmesan cheese	125 mL

1. Bring a pot of lightly salted water to a boil.
2. Meanwhile, using a blender or food processor, combine the basil, parsley, marjoram, pine nuts, and garlic and process until finely chopped. Add the Parmesan, Romano and oil, continuing to purée until the mixture is smooth and the oil is mixed in. Transfer to a large skillet.
3. Add the chicken stock to the pesto and stir well. Let simmer for 3 minutes.
4. In the meantime, cook the pasta *al dente*. Drain well and add to the sauce. Toss or stir so that the pasta is well covered with the pesto, and serve garnished with the basil leaves. Sprinkle with Parmesan and serve immediately.

Penne alla Vodka
(PENNE IN A VODKA SAUCE)

They say that vodka is an odorless liquor, but it is definitely not lacking in taste. Mixed with the savory flavors of this recipe, it will warm your heart and satisfy your stomach.

Makes 4 to 6 servings

3 tbsp	butter	45 mL
3	shallots, finely chopped	3
3	cloves garlic, finely chopped	3
1	ITALPASTA 14-oz (398 mL) tin of plum tomatoes, drained of juice, puréed or finely chopped	1
pinch	salt	pinch
¼ tsp	white pepper	1 mL
pinch	cayenne	pinch
⅓ cup	vodka	75 mL
1 cup	whipping cream	250 mL
¼ tsp	nutmeg	1 mL
⅓ cup	Parmesan cheese, freshly grated	75 mL
2 tbsp	fresh parsley, finely chopped additional Parmesan cheese	25 mL
1 lb	ITALPASTA Penne	500 g

1. Bring a large pot of lightly salted water to a boil.
2. In a large skillet, melt the butter, add the shallots and garlic and sauté briefly over medium heat. When the garlic is golden, add the tomatoes, salt, pepper and cayenne and let simmer until most of the liquid evaporates.
3. Add the vodka, cook for 10 seconds, then add the cream and nutmeg. Stir in the Parmesan cheese and simmer for about 2 minutes or until the sauce begins to thicken. Remove from the heat and set aside.
4. When the water is boiling, add the pasta, cook *al dente*, and drain well. Return the saucepan to the stove, add the pasta to the skillet, toss or stir well and serve sprinkled with the parsley and Parmesan cheese.

Spaghetti alla Puttanesca
(SPAGHETTI WITH ANCHOVIES AND OLIVES)

This dish, using basic and readily available ingredients, is an example of simple country fare.

Makes 4 to 6 servings

3 tbsp	ITALPASTA olive oil	45 mL
2	cloves garlic, finely chopped	2
1	sweet red pepper, diced into ¼-inch (5 mm) pieces	1
½ cup	ITALPASTA tinned anchovies, finely chopped with the oil	125 g
½ cup	black olives, pitted and halved	125 g
2 tbsp	capers	25 mL
1	ITALPASTA 28-oz (796 mL) tin plum tomatoes, diced with the juice	1
1 tsp	ITALPASTA tomato paste	5 mL
2 tbsp	fresh basil	25 mL
1 tbsp	oregano	15 mL
1 tsp	thyme	5 mL
pinch	salt	pinch
¼ tsp	pepper	1 mL
1 lb	ITALPASTA Spaghetti	500 g
	Parmesan cheese, freshly grated	

1. Heat the oil in a large skillet. Add the garlic and red pepper and sauté until the garlic is sizzling. Add the anchovies, stir well, and then add the olives, capers, tomatoes, tomato paste, basil, oregano, thyme, salt, and pepper. Mix well and allow to simmer for 20 minutes until the sauce is reduced and begins to thicken slightly, stirring frequently.
2. Meanwhile, cook the pasta *al dente* in a large pot of boiling salted water. Drain the pasta and add it to the sauce. Mix well and simmer for 1 to 2 minutes.
3. With a fork, put the pasta on a serving dish or individual plates and pour the sauce over top. Sprinkle with Parmesan and serve immediately.

Spaghetti alla Marinara di Sicilia
(SPAGHETTI WITH OLIVES, CAPERS, AND PROSCIUTTO)

Marinara sometimes refers to a sauce with seafood. Create this tomato sauce in your pan with simple and flavorful treasures like kalamata olives and capers.

Makes 4 servings

3 tbsp	ITALPASTA olive oil	45 mL
¼ lb	prosciutto, diced into ¼-inch (5 mm) thick pieces	125 g
1	medium onion, diced	1
4	cloves garlic, finely chopped	4
4 tbsp	fresh basil, finely chopped	50 mL
3 tbsp	capers	45 mL
½ cup	kalamata olives, pitted and sliced	125 mL
¼ cup	dry red wine	50 mL
1 tsp	ITALPASTA tomato paste	5 mL
6	plum tomatoes, peeled, seeded, and diced	6
1 tsp	sugar	5 mL
pinch	salt	pinch
¼ tsp	pepper	1 mL
½ lb	ITALPASTA Spaghetti,	250 g
	Romano cheese, freshly grated	
	fresh basil leaves	
	extra olives for garnish	

1. Bring a large pot of lightly salted water to a boil.
2. In a large skillet, heat the oil and add the prosciutto. Sauté until brown. Add the onion and garlic and continue to sauté until the onion begins to brown. Take care not to burn the garlic.
3. Add the capers and olives, toss or stir, and add the red wine, tomato paste, diced tomatoes, and sugar. Season with salt and pepper. Let the sauce simmer for about 5 or 6 minutes. (If the sauce is too thick, add a little more red wine and simmer for another moment.)
4. When the water is at a strong boil, add the pasta and cook *al dente*. Drain the pasta well, then add to the sauce. Toss or stir well, and cook for another moment until the pasta is well coated and has absorbed some of the sauce.
5. Serve immediately, sprinkled with freshly grated Romano cheese and garnished with basil leaves and olives.

CHAPTER FIVE

Rice & Eggs

Rice

A true risotto is a labor of love. It requires slow cooking and constant, gentle stirring to coax the rice, liquid, and other ingredients to merge into a consistency Italians describe as "all'onda" — "with waves." Inside, the rice will be a little firm. Outside, the grains will be bound in a creamy, flavorful base. Close your eyes and enjoy the rich concentration of tastes and sensuous contrast of textures in this ultimate comfort food.

Eggs

As every cook knows, eggs are a wonder food. They are highly nutritious, easy to store, inexpensive, and tremendously versatile. Aside from their essential but supporting role in many sauces, soups, and baked goods, eggs just as easily take center stage. Mix them with herbs, cheese, or vegetables and you have a quick, easy, and delicious meal.

Risotto alla Fiorentina

(RISOTTO WITH MEAT AND SPINACH)

In many cultures, rice is used as a side dish. In Italy, risotto is eaten as the first or main course. Thus, the risotto is never served alone. The rice should have a creamy consistency. It should be moist, yet the grains should be *al dente*. I love the addition of spinach to this risotto recipe. It is both healthy and colorful.

Makes 4 to 6 servings

2 tbsp	ITALPASTA olive oil	25 mL
2 tbsp	butter, divided	25 mL
1	medium onion, diced	1
¼ lb	lean ground beef	125 g
¼ lb	lean ground pork	125 g
¼ lb	chicken livers, cut into small pieces	125 g
1	large bunch of spinach, washed and stems removed, then torn into pieces	1
pinch	salt	pinch
¼ tsp	black pepper, freshly ground	1 mL
½ tsp	nutmeg	2 mL
1	ITALPASTA 14-oz (398 mL) tin of plum tomatoes with its juice, cut into small pieces	1
2½ cups	ITALPASTA Arborio Rice	625 mL
4 cups	beef or chicken stock (pages 120, 123)	1 L
⅓ cup	Parmesan cheese, freshly grated	75 mL

1. Heat the oil and half of the butter in a medium-sized pot and sauté the onion until golden. Add the beef, pork, and chicken livers and, over medium-high heat, continue to cook until the meat begins to brown. Add the spinach, salt, pepper, and nutmeg and continue to cook, stirring often, until the spinach begins to wilt.
2. Add the tomatoes and adjust seasoning if necessary. Continue to cook on medium heat for about 20 minutes or until most of the liquid is reduced.
3. Stir in the rice and half the stock. Cook for 20 minutes, stirring frequently, and add the remaining stock to moisten as needed.
4. When the risotto is done, remove from the heat and stir in the remaining butter and Parmesan cheese, folding gently. Let stand for 3 to 5 minutes, then serve.

Risotto alla Milanese

(RISOTTO WITH MEAT)

Although risotto is generally served as a meal by itself or as a first course, this dish is traditionally serve with the famous "Osso Bucco" (Beef Shank).

Makes 4 to 6 servings

2 tbsp	ITALPASTA olive oil	25 mL
2 tbsp	butter, divided	25 mL
1	medium onion, diced	1
½ lb	minced beef	250 g
¼ lb	chicken kidney, sliced	125 g
¼ lb	chicken liver, sliced	125 g
1	ITALPASTA 14-oz (398 mL) tin plum tomatoes, seeded and diced	1
pinch	salt	pinch
¼ tsp	black pepper, freshly ground	1 mL
2½ cups	ITALPASTA Arborio Rice	625 mL
4 cups	beef stock (page 120) or broth, divided	1 L
⅓ cup	Parmesan cheese, freshly grated	75 mL

1. Heat the oil and half the butter in a large pot. Add the onion and sauté unt golden. Add the beef, kidney, and liver. Continue to cook over medium-hig heat until the meat is brown.
2. Add the tomatoes, salt, and pepper and let simmer for about 10 minutes or until the sauce begins to thicken.
3. Stir in the rice and half the stock. Cook for about 20 minutes, stirring frequently, and adding more stock as necessary to keep the rice moist.
4. Remove from the heat, stir in the remaining butter, and gently fold in the Parmesan cheese. Let stand for 3 minutes and serve.

Risotto con Asparagi e Zafferano
(RISOTTO WITH ASPARAGUS AND SAFFRON)

I have many times stated my love for asparagus, I offer you this recipe with asparagus and saffron.

Makes 4 to 6 servings

2 tbsp	ITALPASTA olive oil	25 mL
2 tbsp	butter, divided	25 mL
1	medium onion, diced	1
1½ lb	fresh asparagus cut into 1-inch (2.5 cm) pieces, tips separate	750 g
½ cup	dry white wine	125 mL
2 cups	ITALPASTA Arborio Rice	500 mL
¼ tsp	saffron	1 mL
6 cups	chicken stock (page 123) or broth, divided	1.5 L
¼ tsp	salt	1 mL
¼ tsp	black pepper, freshly ground	1 mL
2	large sweet red peppers, diced into ¼-inch (5 mm) pieces	2
3 tbsp	heavy cream	45 mL
⅓ cup	Parmesan cheese, freshly grated	75 mL

In a medium-sized pot, heat the olive oil and half the butter over medium heat and sauté the onion until golden.

Add the asparagus pieces (not the tips) and toss or stir well. Add the wine and simmer for 1 minute.

Add the rice and the saffron and toss or stir well so that the rice is coated with the oil. Add half the chicken stock, stir well, season with salt and pepper, and cook for 20 to 25 minutes, adding the remainder of the stock slowly. After the first 10 minutes, add the asparagus tips and the red peppers.

When the rice is done, remove the pot from the stove and add the remaining butter, cream, and Parmesan cheese. Let stand for 5 minutes and serve.

Risotto con Frutti di Mare al Cognac
(RISOTTO WITH SEAFOOD AND COGNAC)

Some might say: "Why waste a beautiful cognac with a rice dish?" Well, when you adorn it with the wonderful fruits of the sea, what better complement could there be?

Makes 4 to 6 servings

2 tbsp	ITALPASTA extra virgin olive oil	25 mL
2 tbsp	butter, divided	25 mL
1	medium red onion, julienne*	1
3	cloves garlic, finely chopped	3
2	carrots, finely diced	2
1	stalk celery, finely diced	1
½ lb	bay scallops	250 g
½ lb	shrimp, peeled, deveined, and cut in half	250 g
½ lb	swordfish, cut the same size as the scallops	250 g
¼ tsp	salt	1 mL
¼ tsp	black pepper, freshly ground	1 mL
1 tsp	Spanish paprika	5 mL
¼ cup	cognac	50 mL
¼ cup	dry white wine	50 mL
2 cups	ITALPASTA Arborio Rice	500 mL
6 cups	chicken stock (page 123), divided	1.5 L
⅓ cup	Parmesan cheese	75 mL
2 tbsp	fresh parsley, finely chopped	25 mL
2 tbsp	fresh basil, finely chopped	25 mL

*Julienne is strips 2 inches (5 cm) long by ¼ inch (5 mm) wide

1. In a medium-sized pot, heat the olive oil and half the butter over medium heat and sauté the onion until golden. Turn down the heat and add the garlic, carrots, and celery and continue to sauté for another moment or two.
2. Add the scallops, shrimp, and swordfish and season with salt, pepper, and paprika. Increase the heat slightly and toss or stir well. Add the cognac and white wine, sauté for another moment or until the shrimp begin to turn red.
3. Add the rice and mix well so that the rice is coated with the oil.
4. Add half the chicken stock and simmer slowly for about 20 minutes, adding the remainder of the stock little by little until the rice is done.
5. Remove from the heat and add the remainder of the butter, Parmesan cheese, parsley, and basil. Fold in gently, let stand for 3 to 5 minutes, and serve.

Risotto con Gamberetti
(RISOTTO WITH SHRIMP)

How could I overlook a risotto with my favorite seafood?

Makes 4 servings

2 tbsp	ITALPASTA olive oil	25 mL
1	small onion, diced	1
2 cups	ITALPASTA Arborio Rice	500 mL
1 cup	dry white wine	250 mL
6 cups	chicken stock (page 123), divided	1.5 L
2 tbsp	butter	25 mL
3	cloves garlic, finely chopped	3
2 cups	mushrooms, sliced	500 mL
1 lb	medium-to-large shrimp, shell on and deveined	500 g
4	sprigs fresh parsley, finely chopped	4
1	medium green pepper, diced	1
pinch	salt	pinch
pinch	pepper	pinch

1. Heat the oil in a medium-sized pot. Add half the onion and sauté until tender. Add the rice and stir until it is coated with oil. Add ½ cup (125 mL) of wine and 1 cup (250 mL) of stock. Bring to a gentle boil and continue stirring until the liquid is absorbed. Slowly add 4¾ cup (1175 mL) more of the chicken stock and continue to stir frequently until the rice is tender but firm, about 20 minutes. Place the lid on to retain heat and set aside.
2. Heat the butter in a skillet and add the garlic and remaining onion. Sauté until tender and add the mushrooms. Continue to sauté on medium heat until the mushrooms are soft. Add the shrimp and continue to sauté until they begin to turn red, about 1 to 2 minutes. Add the remaining wine, chicken stock, and half of the chopped parsley. Simmer for another 1 to 2 minutes, or until the shrimp are firm.
3. Mix the shrimp and sauce with the rice in a large bowl and serve garnished with the remaining parsley, salt, and pepper.

Risotto con Funghi
(RISOTTO WITH WILD MUSHROOMS)

What better dish than an Italian version of mushroom fried rice! Make the risotto with readily available wild mushrooms, this simple dish becomes as wild as the mushrooms themselves.

Makes 4 to 6 servings

½ cup	dried porcini mushrooms, sliced	125 mL
2 cups	water	500 mL
3 tbsp	butter, divided	45 mL
1	medium onion, finely diced	1
2	cloves garlic, finely chopped	2
2½ cups	ITALPASTA Arborio Rice	625 mL
4 cups	chicken stock (page 123), divided	1 L
2 tbsp	ITALPASTA extra virgin olive oil	25 mL
1 cup	shiitake mushrooms, sliced	250 mL
1 cup	oyster mushrooms, sliced	250 mL
1 cup	portobello mushrooms, sliced into small pieces or the same size as the other mushrooms	250 mL
1 tbsp	fresh basil, finely chopped	15 mL
¼ tsp	salt	1 mL
¼ tsp	pepper	1 mL
1 cup	dry white wine	250 mL
½ cup	Parmesan cheese, freshly grated	125 mL
2 tbsp	fresh parsley, finely chopped green onions	25 mL

1. Soak the porcini mushrooms in 2 cups (500 mL) of luke warm water for 20 to 30 minutes. Remove the mushrooms with a slotted spoon and set aside. Strain the liquid and set aside for cooking the rice.
2. In a medium-sized pot, add 2 tbsp (25 mL) of butter and sauté the onion and garlic until the onion is golden. Be careful not to burn the garlic. Stir in the rice so that it is well coated. Begin to add the stock, half at first and then the remainder, little by little, stirring frequently. Add the mushroom liquid as needed to finish the rice, about 20 minutes.
3. Add the remainder of the butter and the olive oil to a medium-sized skillet and, over medium-high heat, sauté the shiitake, oyster, and portobello mushrooms for 2 to 3 minutes, until they are soft and smaller in size. Add the porcini mushrooms, basil, salt, pepper, and wine. When the wine is reduced by half, remove the skillet from the stove.
4. Add the mushrooms, the liquid in the pan, the Parmesan cheese, and the parsley to the rice. Mix well, taste, and adjust for seasonings. Let stand for 2 to 3 minutes and serve garnished with green onions.

Risotto con Pollo alla Puttanesca
(RISOTTO WITH CHICKEN, CAPERS, BLACK OLIVES, AND ANCHOVY)

Risotto is a very traditional dish in North Italian cuisine. Although my roots are in Southern Italy, I still appreciate a great risotto. This is one of my favorites.

Makes 4 to 6 servings

2 tbsp	ITALPASTA extra virgin olive oil	25 mL
1	medium onion, diced	1
3	cloves garlic, finely chopped	3
1½ lb	boneless chicken cut into 1½-inch (4 cm) by ¼-inch (5 mm) strips	750 g
¼ tsp	salt	1 mL
¼ tsp	black pepper, freshly ground	1 mL
6	anchovy fillets, finely chopped	6
2 tbsp	capers	25 mL
12	black olives, pitted and sliced	12
2 cups	ITALPASTA plum tomatoes, seeded and diced	500 mL
2 tbsp	fresh rosemary	25 mL
2 cups	ITALPASTA Arborio Rice	500 mL
5 cups	chicken stock (page 123), divided	1.25 L
⅓ cup	Parmesan cheese, freshly grated	75 mL
2 tbsp	butter	25 mL
3 tbsp	fresh parsley, finely chopped	45 mL

1. Using a medium-sized pot, heat the oil and sauté the onion until golden. Add the garlic and chicken pieces, season with salt and pepper, and continue to sauté, stirring frequently until the chicken begins to brown and is about half cooked.
2. Add the anchovy, capers, and black olives and continue to cook, tossing or stirring frequently, for 2 minutes. Stir in the tomatoes and the rosemary. Simmer for 2 minutes or until any excess liquid is reduced.
3. Add the rice. Using a wooden spoon, mix all the ingredients. Add half of the chicken stock and cook the risotto for about 20 minutes, adding the remainder of the stock slowly as needed.
4. When the risotto is cooked, remove from the heat and fold in the Parmesan cheese, butter, and chopped parsley. Let stand for 3 to 5 minutes and serve.

Frittata con Spaghettini (see page

Frittata con Spaghettini

(FRITTATA WITH SPAGHETTINI, ZUCCHINI, EGGPLANT, AND MUSHROOMS)

A green salad with a little olive oil and red wine vinegar served with this frittata makes a wonderful weekend brunch.

Makes 4 to 6 servings

½ lb	ITALPASTA Spaghettini	250 g
2 tbsp	ITALPASTA olive oil	25 mL
2 tbsp	sweet butter	25 mL
1	medium onion, julienne*	1
1½ cups	mushrooms, sliced	375 mL
1	clove garlic, finely chopped	1
1	small zucchini, cut into ¼-inch (5 mm) rounds	1
1	small eggplant, diced	1
4	plum tomatoes, seeded and diced	4
1 tbsp	fresh basil, coarsely chopped	15 mL
1 tbsp	oregano	15 mL
pinch	salt	pinch
pinch	pepper	pinch
8	eggs	8
½ cup	mozzarella cheese, grated and divided	125 mL
¼ cup	Parmesan cheese, grated and divided	50 mL
	basil for garnish	
	tomato slices for garnish	

Julienne is strips 2 inches (5 cm) long by ¼ inch (5 mm) wide

1. Preheat the oven to 350°F (180°C).
2. Bring a large pot of lightly salted water to a boil, add pasta, and cook *al dente*. Rinse in cold water and drain well.
3. Heat oil and butter in an ovenproof skillet, sauté the onion and mushrooms, stirring frequently until the excess liquid is evaporated. Add the garlic and sauté on medium heat for 1 minute.
4. Add the zucchini, eggplant, tomatoes, basil, oregano, salt, and pepper to taste and continue to cook on medium heat until the excess liquid is evaporated and the vegetables are tender.
5. Beat eggs in a large bowl and add the cooked pasta, half of the mozzarella, and half of the Parmesan; mix thoroughly. Add this mixture to the skillet and combine evenly with the egg and vegetable mixture. Cook over medium-low heat until the bottom of the frittata is set. Sprinkle the top with the remaining cheese and place the skillet in the oven until the egg is set and the cheese is lightly browned. Remove from heat and let stand for 2 to 3 minutes. Divide into portions and serve garnished with basil and a slice of tomato.

Frittata con Ruòte, Spinaci, e Menta

(FRITTATA WITH SPINACH, MINT, AND WAGON WHEEL PASTA)

Although not commonly used with eggs, mint is a refreshingly aromatic addition to this light and fluffy dish. Ideal for lunch or Sunday brunch.

Makes 4 servings

½ lb	ITALPASTA Wagon Wheel pasta	250 g
2 tbsp	butter	25 mL
1	medium leek (white part only), diced	1
1 cup	cooked spinach (with the excess water squeezed out), chopped	250 mL
6	mint leaves, coarsely chopped	6
8	whole eggs, beaten with ¼ cup (50 mL) milk and a pinch of salt and pepper	8
2 tbsp	parsley, chopped	25 mL
2 tbsp	Parmesan cheese, freshly grated	25 mL
pinch	salt	pinch
pinch	black pepper, freshly ground (optional)	pinch

1. Preheat the oven to 375°F (190°C).
2. Bring a large pot of lightly salted water to a boil. Add pasta and cook *al dente*. Rinse in cold water and drain well.
3. Using an ovenproof skillet with high sides, melt the butter over medium he Add the leek and spinach and sauté for 1 to 2 minutes. Add the mint and t or stir until the mixture is well coated.
4. Add half the egg mixture and, with a rubber spatula, stir the mixture so tha the eggs and spinach are combined. Cook over medium-low heat until it begins to set.
5. Mix the parsley with the remaining egg. Place the pasta over the partially cooked egg in the skillet and pour the remaining eggs onto the pasta. Sprinkle with Parmesan cheese.
6. Place in the oven for 10 to 15 minutes or until the top is browned. The inside should be cooked and fluffy. Remove from the oven, let stand for 2 to 3 minutes, and serve.

CHAPTER SIX

Baked & Stuffed Pasta

There is nothing like presenting a sizzling, layered

lasagna or a platter of bright red stuffed peppers to your

guests to make their mouths water. These recipes require a

little more time and effort than many others but they tell

your friends and family that you care enough to go to

the trouble.

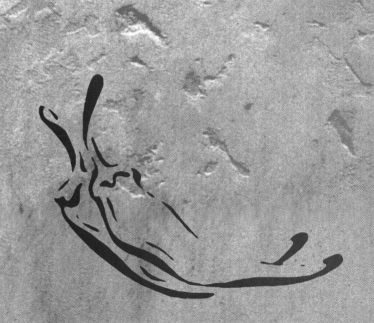

Cannelloni di Mare alla Béchamel

(Cannelloni Stuffed with Seafood and Spinach in a White Sauce)

If you are a seafood lover as I am, you're always looking for different ways to prepare it. This recipe can be made ahead of time or even frozen then defrosted and served when you like.

Makes 4 to 6 Servings

16	**ITALPASTA Oven Ready Cannelloni**	16
3 to 4	**bunches of fresh spinach, washed, with stem off (about 1 pound/500 g)**	3 to 4
1 lb	**fresh crab meat, chopped**	500 g
1 lb	**baby shrimp, cooked**	500 g
1 tbsp	**ITALPASTA olive oil**	15 mL
1 tbsp	**butter**	15 mL
1	**medium onion, diced**	1
3	**cloves garlic, finely chopped**	3
3 cups	**béchamel sauce (page 122)**	750 mL
2	**whole eggs**	2
2 tbsp	**bread crumbs**	25 mL
¼ tsp	**salt**	1 mL
¼ tsp	**pepper**	1 mL
1 tsp	**nutmeg, grated**	5 mL
1 cup	**Parmesan cheese, freshly grated**	250 mL
2 tbsp	**fresh parsley, finely chopped**	25 mL
3	**sprigs parsley flowers**	3

1. Preheat oven to 350°F (180°C).
2. Steam the spinach in boiling water, covered, for 2 to 3 minutes. Drain and rinse with cold water, then squeeze out the excess water by hand. Chop the spinach finely.
3. In a large bowl, mix the chopped crab meat, baby shrimp, and spinach.
4. Heat the oil and butter in a frying pan, sauté the onion and garlic.
5. Add the onion and garlic to the seafood mixture, then add 1 cup (250 mL) béchamel sauce, eggs, bread crumbs, salt, pepper, and nutmeg. Mix these ingredients thoroughly. If the mixture appears too loose or runny, add more bread crumbs until it is firm but still moist.
6. Stuff a portion of the seafood mixture into each cannelloni.
7. Cover the bottom of a casserole dish with ½ to 1 cup (125 to 250 mL) of the white sauce and place the cannelloni in the dish, side by side. Cover the cannelloni with the remaining béchamel sauce and sprinkle with the Parmesan cheese.
8. Bake for about 20 minutes or until the sauce is bubbling. Sprinkle with chopped parsley and garnish with parsley flowers.

Lasagne di Spinaci con Frutti di Mare
(SPINACH LASAGNA WITH ASSORTED SEAFOOD)

Lasagna does not have to be a basic meat or vegetable dish, and certainly does not have to be ordinary. You can use any type of fish or seafood for this lasagna. You are limited only by your imagination.

Makes 6 servings

1½ lb	ITALPASTA Spinach Lasagna	750 g
2 tbsp	butter	25 mL
5	shallots, finely diced	5
3	cloves garlic, finely minced	3
1 lb	shrimp, medium sized	500 g
½ lb	bay scallops	250 g
½ lb	fresh crab meat cut to the size of the scallops	250 g
2	5-oz (142 g) cans smoked oysters, drained	2
½ cup	dry white wine	125 mL
2 cups	béchamel sauce (page 122)	500 mL
1½ cups	tomato sauce (page 121)	375 mL
1 lb	mozzarella, thinly sliced	500 g
½ cup	Parmesan cheese, freshly grated	125 mL
3 tbsp	fresh parsley, chopped	45 mL

Preheat the oven to 375°F (190°C).

Bring a large pot of lightly salted water to a boil. Cook lasagna *al dente*, rinse in cold water, drain, and lay flat on a tea towel.

Heat the butter in a large skillet and sauté the shallots and garlic. Add the seafood and continue to sauté over medium heat for 1 minute. Add the white wine and reduce by half or until the shrimp are half cooked (about 1 minute). Add the béchamel to the seafood mixture, stir well, and set aside. If the sauce seems too thick, add a little extra white wine.

In a baking dish (9-inch x 13-inch x 3-inch/3.5 L), dot the bottom with the tomato sauce, then add a layer of lasagna, a layer of the seafood mixture, dots of the tomato sauce, a layer of the mozzarella cheese, then repeat: lasagna, seafood mixture, dots of tomato sauce, mozzarella cheese, and once more. These ingredients should give you 3 to 4 layers, the last layer being the seafood mixture, dotted with the remaining tomato sauce.

Sprinkle well with the Parmesan cheese and bake uncovered for 20 to 30 minutes or until the sauce is bubbling. Let stand for 10 minutes, sprinkle with the parsley, and serve.

Maccheroni al Forno alla Rustica
(BAKED ELBOW PASTA WITH EGGPLANT AND MOZZARELLA)

If you are a lover of eggplant and like a light, meatless meal, this is one to try.

Makes 4 to 6 servings

1 lb	ITALPASTA Elbow Pasta	500 g
	vegetable oil	
1	large eggplant, peeled and cut into ¼-inch (5 mm) thick slices	1
4 tbsp	butter, divided	50 mL
1	medium onion, thinly sliced	1
1	ITALPASTA 28-oz (796 mL) tin plum tomatoes with juice, coarsely chopped	1
3 tbsp	fresh basil, coarsely chopped	45 mL
¼ tsp	salt	1 mL
¼ tsp	black pepper, freshly ground	1 mL
¼ cup	Parmesan cheese, freshly grated	50 mL
⅓ lb	mozzarella cheese, thinly sliced	170 g
	additional Parmesan cheese	
2 tbsp	fresh parsley, finely chopped	25 mL

1. Preheat the oven to 350°F (180°C).
2. Bring a large pot of lightly salted water to a boil. Add the pasta and cook *molto al dente*. Drain well.
3. Pour vegetable oil into a skillet until it comes ½ inch (1 cm) up the side. When the oil is hot, put as many eggplant slices in the oil as will fit. Cook both sides, turning them over as the bottom side browns. Transfer them to a plate covered with paper towels. Set aside.
4. Pour the oil from the skillet into a glass jar after it has cooled. Add the butter to the skillet, reserving about 1 tsp (5 mL) for later use. Sauté the onion until golden. Add the tomatoes, basil, salt, and pepper and simmer until the sauce is reduced and is not watery. Remove from the heat. Add the pasta to the sauce with the Parmesan cheese. Toss or stir well, then set aside.
5. Smear the bottom of a baking dish with the remaining butter and put in about half the pasta, spreading it evenly. Cover with the eggplant slices and a layer of the mozzarella cheese. Put in the remaining pasta, cover with the remaining mozzarella cheese (add more if necessary so that all of the pasta is covered with cheese). Sprinkle with the additional Parmesan cheese and bake for 15 to 20 minutes or until the top has browned.
6. Remove from the oven and let stand for 5 to 10 minutes, then serve sprinkled with parsley.

Lumache Ripiene al Forno

(BAKED PASTA SHELLS STUFFED WITH RICOTTA AND VEGETABLES)

Ricotta, a wonderful and moist cheese, is great mixed with other delicacies and stuffed into any pasta like cannelloni or manicotti and then baked. Adorn with a tomato sauce and what you have is a wonderful summertime, or anytime, meatless meal.

Makes 4 to 6 servings

16	**ITALPASTA Jumbo Shells**	16
1 tbsp	**ITALPASTA olive oil**	15 mL
2 tbsp	**butter**	25 mL
1	**medium onion, finely diced**	1
3	**cloves garlic, finely minced**	3
2 cups	**mushrooms, quartered**	500 mL
1	**red pepper, diced into ¼-inch (5 mm) pieces**	1
1	**yellow pepper, diced into ¼-inch, (5 mm) pieces**	1
1	**green pepper, diced into ¼-inch, (5 mm) pieces**	1
1½ lb	**ricotta cheese**	750 g
1	**egg, well beaten**	1
½ cup	**Parmesan cheese, freshly grated**	125 mL
3 tbsp	**fresh basil, finely chopped**	45 mL
4 tbsp	**fresh parsley, chopped**	50 mL
½ tsp	**oregano**	2 mL
¼ tsp	**salt**	1 mL
¼ tsp	**white pepper**	1 mL
	bread crumbs	
3 cups	**tomato sauce (page 121)**	750 mL
	additional Parmesan cheese	

1. Preheat the oven to 375°F (190°C).
2. In a large pot of lightly salted water, cook the pasta shells *al dente*. Remove with a slotted spoon, immerse in a pot of cold water, then place on a paper towel to dry. Set aside.
3. Heat the oil and butter in a large saucepan over medium heat, sauté the onion, garlic, and mushrooms. Add the peppers and continue to sauté until they begin to cook, but are still crunchy. Place in a bowl and allow to cool room temperature.
4. When the vegetable mixture is cool, add the ricotta, egg, Parmesan, basil, the parsley, oregano, salt, and white pepper. Mix well. If the mixture is too moist, add a little more Parmesan or bread crumbs or a combination of both until it is firm but still moist.
5. Line the bottom of a large baking dish with enough tomato sauce to thinly cover it. Gently stuff the cooked pasta shells with the ricotta mixture and place them in the baking dish side by side. Spoon a little sauce over each shell and sprinkle with Parmesan cheese.
6. Bake the shells for about 30 minutes or until the sauce is bubbling and the cheese mixture is hot. Let stand for 10 to 15 minutes and serve with additio Parmesan cheese.

Manicotti alla Fiorentina

(MANICOTTI WITH RICOTTA AND SPINACH)

s dish and a fresh garden salad with an oil and vinegar dressing make a wonderful light weekend
nch. Serve hot or at room temperature.

kes 4 servings

12	**ITALPASTA Manicotti**	12
⅓ **lb**	spinach	170 g
1 **lb**	ricotta cheese	500 g
¼ cup	Romano cheese, freshly grated	50 mL
2	eggs	2
1 tbsp	flour	15 mL
2 tbsp	bread crumbs	25 mL
½ tsp	nutmeg	2 mL
¼ tsp	salt	1 mL
pinch	pepper	pinch
1 cup	tomato sauce (page 121)	250 mL
1 cup	béchamel sauce (page 122)	250 mL

Preheat the oven to 350°F (180°F).

Bring a pot of lightly salted water to a boil. Add the manicotti and cook *al
dente*. Rinse in cold water, drain, and place on a tea towel.

Cook the spinach so that it is limp, but has not lost any colour. Rinse in cold
water and, with your hands, squeeze out the excess water. Chop finely.

Add the spinach to the ricotta, then add the Romano cheese, eggs, flour, bread
crumbs, nutmeg, salt, and pepper. Mix well. If the mixture is too moist, add
more bread crumbs and Romano cheese a little at a time until it is firmer, then
stuff the manicotti with this mixture.

Spread half of the tomato sauce on the bottom of a baking dish and place the
manicotti on top. Cover with the remaining sauce and cover again with the
béchamel. Bake for 10 to 15 minutes or until the sauces are bubbling. Let
stand for 5 minutes and serve.

Manicotti alla Romana

(MANICOTTI WITH A MEAT STUFFING)

This dish requires a little time to prepare, but is well worth the effort. A delicious main course, it also
makes an excellent appetizer.

Makes 4 to 6 servings

16	**ITALPASTA Manicotti**	16
3 tbsp	vegetable oil	45 mL
½ **lb each**	veal, beef, pork, all cubed	250 g
1	celery stalk, cut into chunky pieces	1
1	medium onion, cut into chunky pieces	1
1	large carrot, cut into chunky pieces	1
2	cloves garlic, coarsely chopped	2
¼ cup	dry white wine	50 mL
1 tbsp	brandy	15 mL
3	large plum tomatoes, peeled, seeded, and chopped	3
2	bunches spinach	2
½ cup	chicken stock (page 123)	125 mL
pinch	salt	pinch
¼ tsp	pepper	1 mL
¼ tsp	nutmeg	1 mL
2	bay leaves	2
2	egg yolks	2
½ cup	Parmesan cheese, grated and divided	125 mL
1½ cups	tomato sauce (page 121)	375 mL
½ cup	béchamel (page 122)	125 mL

1. Preheat oven to 350°F (180°C).
2. Bring a pot of lightly salted water to a boil. Add manicotti and cook *al dente*.
   Rinse in cold water, drain, and place on a tea towel.
3. In a large skillet, heat the oil and sauté the veal, beef, pork, celery, onion,
   carrots, and garlic until brown, stirring frequently.
4. Transfer to a roasting pan and add the wine, brandy, tomatoes, spinach,
   chicken stock, salt, pepper, nutmeg, and bay leaves. Cover and bake until the
   meat is tender, about 20 to 30 minutes.
5. Allow to cool, remove the bay leaves, and run mixture through a meat grinder
   with a fine attachment or purée using a food processor. Add the egg yolk and
   ¼ cup (50 mL) of Parmesan cheese. Blend well. The stuffing should be very
   smooth, with no lumps.
6. Stuff the manicotti. Spoon some of the tomato sauce into a baking dish. Place
   the manicotti in the dish and spoon a little of the béchamel sauce over each.
   Cover with the remaining tomato sauce and sprinkle with the remaining
   Parmesan cheese. Bake uncovered for 10 to 15 minutes and serve.

nicotti alla Fiorentina

Peperoni Ripiene con Nochette, Funghi, e Carciofi

(STUFFED RED PEPPERS WITH SMALL BOW TIES, WILD MUSHROOMS, AND ARTICHOKES)

The meaty texture of the wild mushrooms and the variety of flavors and herbs make this dish a satisfying vegetarian treat.

Makes 6 servings

1 lb	**ITALPASTA Small Bow Ties**	500 g
6	**large red peppers (with stem), cut in half**	6
3 tbsp	**butter**	45 mL
4	**shallots, finely diced**	4
3	**cloves garlic, finely chopped**	3
1 cup	**each shiitake mushrooms, oyster mushrooms, portobello mushrooms, coarsely chopped**	250 mL
1	**14-oz (398 mL) tin artichoke hearts, diced into small pieces**	1
1 tsp	**oregano**	5 mL
1 tsp	**thyme**	5 mL
1 tsp	**rosemary**	5 mL
¼ tsp	**salt**	1 mL
¼ tsp	**pepper**	1 mL
½ cup	**dry white wine**	125 mL
6	**plum tomatoes, peeled, seeded, and diced finely**	6
½ cup	**combined freshly grated Romano, freshly grated Parmesan, bread crumbs**	125 mL
	additional Romano cheese for garnish	
	parsley for garnish	

1. Preheat oven to 375°F (190°C).
2. Cook the pasta *molto al dente*, rinse in cold water, drain, and set aside.
3. In a large skillet, sauté the shallots and garlic until clear. Add the mushrooms, artichoke, oregano, thyme, rosemary, salt and pepper. Continue to sauté, tossing or stirring frequently until the mushrooms are soft, about 2 to 3 minutes.
4. Add the wine and diced tomatoes and simmer over medium heat for an additional 5 to 10 minutes or until the sauce is reduced considerably (it should not be runny).
5. Remove from the heat and add the Romano, Parmesan, and enough bread crumbs to absorb the remaining liquid. Add the cooked pasta. Stir well and then stuff each red pepper half to the brim. Place the red pepper halves in a baking dish that has been lightly oiled and bake for 15 to 20 minutes or until the peppers begin to brown. Sprinkle with additional Romano cheese and parsley and serve immediately.

Peperoni Ripiene con Nochette,
Funghi, e Carciofi

Melanzane Ripiene al Forno
(STUFFED BAKED EGGPLANT)

In Italy and throughout Europe, eggplant is a widely used vegetable. Not having a distinct flavor of its own, it takes on the flavors of the ingredients in the dish.

Makes 4 to 6 servings

3 cups	ITALPASTA Orzo (or other small pasta)	750 mL
6	small eggplants	6
2 tbsp	ITALPASTA olive oil	25 mL
1	large red pepper, diced into ¼-inch cubes	1
3 cups	tomato sauce (page 121)	750 mL
½ cup	Parmesan cheese, freshly grated	125 mL
⅓ cup	mozzarella, grated	175 mL
2 tbsp	fresh basil, finely chopped	25 mL
1 tsp	thyme	5 mL
¼ tsp	salt	1 mL
¼ tsp	pepper	1 mL
	additional Parmesan cheese and mozzarella	

1. Preheat the oven to 375°F (190°C).
2. Cook the pasta *al dente* in lightly salted boiling water. Rinse in cold water, drain, and set aside.
3. Cut the eggplant in half. Scoop out the pulp and place in a colander, sprinkle with salt, and allow to drain for about 30 minutes. Squeeze out excess moisture and chop into small pieces.
4. Add the oil to a skillet and sauté the eggplant until it begins to brown. Add the red peppers and sauté for another 2 minutes or until the peppers begin to soften. Remove from heat and place in a large mixing bowl.
5. Add 1 cup (250 mL) tomato sauce, Parmesan cheese, mozzarella, basil, pasta, thyme, salt, and pepper and mix well. Fill the eggplant shells with the mixture.
6. Ladle a small amount of the tomato sauce into a large baking dish and place the stuffed eggplants side by side. Cover with 1 cup (250 mL) of tomato sauce and additional mozzarella and Parmesan cheese. Bake for about 30 minutes or until the tops are lightly browned.

Lasagne alla Primavera al Forno

(LASAGNA WITH ROASTED VEGETABLES)

For the vegetarian, or those who just love vegetables, here is a wonderful dish.

Makes 6 servings

1½ lb	**ITALPASTA Lasagna**	750 g
2 cups	**mushrooms, halved**	500 mL
1	**large sweet red pepper, cut into chunks**	1
1	**large yellow pepper, cut into chunks**	1
1	**large green pepper, cut into chunks**	1
1	**large zucchini, cut into 1-inch (2.5 cm) pieces**	1
2	**red onions, roughly cut**	2
1 cup	**kalamata olives, pitted and cut in half**	250 mL
3 tbsp	**ITALPASTA olive oil**	45 mL
4 tbsp	**fresh basil**	50 mL
1 tsp	**oregano**	5 mL
1 tsp	**rosemary**	5 mL
3	**cloves garlic, finely chopped**	3
pinch	**salt**	pinch
pinch	**pepper, freshly ground**	pinch
2 cups	**tomato sauce (page 121)**	500 mL
1 lb	**mozzarella, thinly sliced**	500 g
¼ cup	**Parmesan cheese, freshly grated**	50 mL

1. Preheat the oven to 450°F (230°C).
2. Bring a large pot of lightly salted water to a boil. Cook lasagna *al dente*, rinse in cold water, drain, and lay flat on a tea towel.
3. In a large mixing bowl, combine mushrooms, peppers, zucchini, onions, and olives. Add the oil, basil, oregano, rosemary, garlic, salt, and black pepper. Mix well so that everything is coated with the oil. Transfer to a roasting pan and bake uncovered for 15 to 20 minutes, or until the vegetables are browned, stirring often.
4. Reduce the oven temperature to 375°F (190°C).
5. Line the bottom of a baking dish (9 inch x 13 inch x 3 inch/3.5 L) with a ladle of tomato sauce. Add a layer of lasagna, a layer of vegetables, a layer of mozzarella, then sauce, pasta, vegetables, cheese and keep repeating until the ingredients are used up (the last layer being the tomato sauce). Sprinkle with Parmesan cheese, additional olives, and a few of the roasted vegetables.
6. Bake uncovered for 20 to 30 minutes or until the sauce is bubbling and the top is brown. Let stand for 10 to 15 minutes and serve.

Lasagne alla Bolognese

(LASAGNA WITH MEAT SAUCE)

There is your basic lasagna and your not-so-basic lasagna. I like it with a lot of sauce and a lot of chee Remember that it is only as good as the sauce that you use. The key to this dish is the construction of lasagna using an oven dish 12 inches by 8 inches by 3 to 4 inches in height (3 L). The simple techniqu the construction is sauce, pasta, cheese, then sauce, pasta, cheese, then sauce, pasta, cheese, then sauc

Makes 6 servings

1½ lb	**ITALPASTA Lasagna**	750 g
4 cups	**Bolognese sauce (page 122)**	1 L
1 lb	**mozzarella cheese, thinly sliced**	500 g
½ lb	**ricotta cheese**	250 g
½ cup	**Parmesan cheese, freshly grated**	125 mL
3 tbsp	**fresh parsley, chopped**	45 mL
	additional Parmesan cheese	

1. Preheat oven to 375°F (190°C).
2. Bring a large pot of lightly salted water to a boil. Cook lasagna *al dente*, ri in cold water, drain, and lay flat on a tea towel.
3. (a) With ½ cup (125 mL) of Bolognese sauce, cover the bottom of the casserole dish; (b) place pasta side by side; (c) add mozzarella cheese and with ricotta cheese. Repeat these steps until the casserole dish is full. The t should be a coating of the sauce.
4. Sprinkle with the Parmesan cheese and bake for 30 to 40 minutes, or until sauce bubbles and the Parmesan has browned. Let stand for 10 to 15 minu and serve sprinkled with parsley and additional Parmesan.

CHAPTER SEVEN

Soups with Pasta

Historically, soups began as a thrifty way to capture

the last bits of flavor and nutrition from yesterday's

bones and vegetables. Since then, making soup has

evolved into an art of its own. Begin with a basic

broth (see Chapter 8). Add tender pieces of meat,

chicken, or seafood, slivers of colorful fresh vegetables,

a pinch of spice or fresh herbs, and a handful of pasta

for body and you have a nutritious appetizer. Serve

with crusty bread and a salad and it becomes a

nutritious, light meal.

Minestra di Ceci

(CHICKPEA [GARBANZO] SOUP WITH TUBETTINI PASTA)

Minestre are substantial soups with either rice or pasta added that are served as either a first course or an entrée. They can be made with leftover or freshly bought meats. Vary the amount of vegetables or other ingredients according to your taste.

Makes 4 servings

1 lb	chickpeas	500 g
1½ cups	ITALPASTA Tubettini pasta (or other small soup pasta) or Arborio Rice	375 mL
¼ lb	raw ham or other cut of boneless pork	125 g
2	cloves garlic	2
1	large carrot, chopped	1
1	celery stalk, chopped	1
3 tbsp	ITALPASTA olive oil	45 mL
½ lb	pork sausage, boiled and diced into ¼-inch (5 mm) pieces	250 g
1	ITALPASTA 28-oz (796 mL) tin plum tomatoes, coarsely chopped with the juice	1
2 cups	chicken stock (page 123) or broth	500 mL
1 cup	water	250 mL
¼ tsp	marjoram	1 mL
2 tbsp	fresh parsley, chopped	25 mL
1	head chicory (endive), leaves only	1
¼ tsp	salt	1 mL
¼ tsp	black pepper, freshly ground	1 mL
6	slices of toasted bread	6
⅓ cup	pecorino cheese, freshly grated	75 mL

1. Put the chickpeas in a large bowl and soak covered in cold water for 24 hours.
2. Bring a pot of lightly salted water to a boil and cook the pasta *al dente*. Rinse in cold water and drain.
3. Mince the pork or ham with the garlic, carrot, and celery. In a large soup pot, add the oil, minced pork mixture, and sausage and sauté until the meat begins to brown, stirring frequently.
4. Drain the chickpeas and add to the pot with the tomatoes, chicken stock, and water. Add the marjoram, parsley, and chicory and bring to a boil.
5. Season with salt and pepper and let simmer partially covered for 1 to 1½ hours. As you are simmering the soup, the excess oil will come to the top. With a soup ladle, periodically skim the oil and discard it.
6. When the soup is ready, add the pecorino cheese and the cooked pasta. Simmer for another minute or two. Place a slice of toast in each soup bowl. Ladle the soup over the toast and serve immediately.

Minestra di Gamberi e Zafferano

(SAFFRON SHRIMP SOUP WITH TUBETTINI)

An aromatic soup that can be served as a first course or an entrée.

Makes 4 servings

1 tbsp	ITALPASTA extra virgin olive oil	15 mL
1 tbsp	butter	15 mL
1	medium onion, diced	1
1	medium carrot, diced	1
¼ cup	dry white wine	50 mL
1 tsp	saffron	5 mL
1 tsp	dried tarragon	5 mL
4 cups	chicken stock (page 123) or broth	1 L
2 cups	fish stock (page 123) or clam juice	500 mL
5	fresh plum tomatoes, seeded and diced	5
¾ cup	ITALPASTA Tubettini	175 mL
1 lb	shrimp, peeled, deveined, and chopped	500 g
1 cup	frozen petite peas, thawed	250 mL
¼ tsp	salt (optional)	1 mL
¼ tsp	pepper (optional)	1 mL
2 tbsp	chives or scallions, chopped	25 mL
pinch	cayenne pepper	pinch

1. Heat the olive oil and butter in a saucepan and sauté the onions and carrot until the onions are clear. Add the wine, saffron, and tarragon and simmer until almost all of the wine is gone.
2. Add the chicken stock, fish stock, and tomatoes and bring to a boil.
3. Add the pasta and cook uncovered for about 5 minutes, stirring frequently. When the pasta is *al dente*, add the shrimp and peas and bring back to a b
4. Season with salt and pepper if needed, and serve garnished with the chives or scallions and cayenne.

Minestra di Mare con Basilico
(BROTH OF SEAFOOD WITH FRESH BASIL)

unlike a bouillabaisse, you can use a variety of seafood in this flavorful broth. The more seafood
ed, the more you will enjoy this hearty meal.

es 6 servings

1½ cups	ITALPASTA Vegetable Small Shells	375 mL
10 cups	chicken stock (page 123) or fish stock (page 123) (The fish stock will have a stronger taste)	2.5 L
2	medium leeks, white and light green parts only, cut thin as a toothpick, 1½ inches (4 cm) long	2
2	medium carrots, thinly cut, 1½ inches (4 cm) long	2
1	small yellow squash, thinly cut, ½ inches (4 cm) long	1
½ cup	dry white wine	125 mL
2 tbsp	red wine vinegar	25 mL
2 tbsp	lemon juice	25 mL
20	fresh basil leaves, cut in half	20
3	bay leaves	3
24	cultured mussels	24
½ lb	medium shrimp, peeled and deveined, cut into halves	250 g
¼ lb	fresh bay scallops	125 g
¼ lb	fillet of sea bass, skinned and cut into spoon-size strips, ¼ inch (5 mm) by 1½ inches (4 cm)	125 g
¼ lb	fillet of red snapper, skinned and cut into spoon-size strips, ¼ inch (5 mm) by 1½ inches (4 cm)	125 g
pinch	salt	pinch
	white pepper to taste	

Bring a pot of lightly salted water to a boil and cook the pasta *al dente*.
Rinse in cold water, drain, and set aside.
Bring the chicken or fish stock to a boil. Add the leeks, carrots, squash, wine,
vinegar, lemon juice, basil, and bay leaf to the broth and let simmer, partially
covered, for 30 minutes.
Add all of the seafood and, over high heat, bring the soup back to a boil.
Season with salt and pepper, then reduce the heat and let simmer for about 5
minutes. Discard any mussels that have not opened. When you stir this soup,
be careful not to break the fish pieces as they are very delicate.
Add the pasta to the soup, remove the bay leaves, and serve immediately.

Minestra di Pasta e Fagioli
(PASTA AND BEAN SOUP)

Although I use kidney beans in this soup, you may use any bean of your choice.

Makes 4 servings

¼ cup	ITALPASTA extra virgin olive oil	50 mL
1	medium yellow onion, finely chopped	1
1 cup	carrots, finely diced	250 mL
1 cup	celery, finely diced	250 mL
3	small pork chops or ribs	3
1 cup	ITALPASTA plum tomatoes with juice, coarsely chopped	250 mL
3 cups	ITALPASTA canned kidney beans or uncooked (after soaking for 30 minutes)	750 mL
4 cups	beef stock (page 120) or 1 beef boullion cube dissolved in 4 cups (1 L) of boiling water	1 L
pinch	salt	pinch
½ lb	ITALPASTA Tubetti	250 g
¼ cup	Parmesan cheese, freshly grated	50 mL
pinch	black pepper, freshly ground	pinch

1. In a large soup pot, add oil and sauté the onions, carrots, and celery over
   medium heat until the onions turn a rich golden color. Add the pork and stir
   occasionally, for about 5 minutes.
2. Add the tomatoes, bring to a boil, reduce the heat, and let simmer, about
   15 minutes.
3. Add the kidney beans, stir well, and add the broth. Simmer for another 5
   minutes if using canned pre-cooked beans, or 35 minutes if using pre-soaked,
   uncooked kidney beans.
4. Remove the pork and, using a slotted spoon, scoop out about a quarter of the
   beans. Purée them in a food processor or mash them with a fork and return
   them to the soup. Season with salt. Then remove the meat from the bone,
   dice the meat, and return it to the soup.
5. At this point, the soup should not be watery but should be liquid enough to
   cook the pasta. Add more broth if necessary and bring to a boil. Add the
   pasta and stir well so that it does not clump.
6. When the pasta is *al dente*, remove the pot from the heat and allow it to rest
   for a few minutes before serving. Serve with freshly grated Parmesan cheese
   and black pepper.

Stracciatella alla Romana
(CHICKEN BROTH WITH EGG AND PARMESAN CHEESE)

The Chinese call it egg drop soup. This traditional Italian soup is simple and one of my favorites.

Makes 6 servings

8 cups	chicken stock (page 123)	2 L
	white pepper to taste	
1½ cups	ITALPASTA Acini de Pepe or any other small soup pasta	375 mL
6	whole eggs	6
½ cup	Parmesan cheese, freshly grated	125 mL
3 tbsp	fresh parsley, finely chopped	45 mL
	salt (optional)	

1. Place the chicken stock in a large soup pot and add the pepper. Bring the broth to a boil and add the pasta. Cook the pasta in the broth, about 5 minutes or less, stirring well so that it does not lump together.
2. Meanwhile, in a medium-sized mixing bowl, add the eggs, Parmesan cheese, and parsley. Using a whisk, mix the ingredients until smooth.
3. When the pasta is almost cooked, add the egg mixture slowly to the simmering broth. Increase the heat and let the broth come back to a boil stirring constantly.
4. Cook for 3 to 5 minutes, then serve with additional parsley and Parmesan cheese. Salt to taste, if desired.

Minestrone alla Romana

When I am not sure what soup to make for a certain evening, I always resort to this recipe. I usually make it a day in advance and reheat it before serving (which is when I add the pasta). Soups always taste better the next day.

Makes 6 to 8 servings

1½ cups	ITALPASTA Elbows	375 mL
3 tbsp	ITALPASTA extra virgin olive oil	45 mL
1	large Spanish onion, diced into ¼-inch (5 mm) pieces	1
3	large carrots, diced into ¼-inch (5 mm) pieces	3
3	stalks celery, diced into ¼-inch (5 mm) pieces	3
1	large potato, diced into ¼-inch (5 mm) pieces	1
4 cups	chicken stock (page 123)	1 L
2	ITALPASTA 28-oz (796 mL) tins plum tomatoes, with juice, cut into small cubes	2
3 tbsp	fresh oregano, chopped	45 mL
3 tbsp	fresh basil, chopped	45 mL
4	bay leaves	4
¼ tsp	salt	1 mL
¼ tsp	black pepper, freshly ground	1 mL
1	19-oz (540 mL) tin kidney beans	1
1	19-oz (540 mL) tin Romano beans	1
1	16-oz (500 mL) package of spinach (stems removed), roughly cut	1
½ lb	asparagus spears (base removed), cut into 1-inch (2.5 cm) pieces	250 g
2	medium zucchini, diced into ¼-inch (5 mm) pieces	2
	Parmesan or Romano cheese, freshly grated	

1. Bring a pot of lightly salted water to a boil and cook the pasta *al dente*. Rinse in cold water, drain, and refrigerate for future use, or set aside for immediate use.
2. In a large soup pot, heat the oil on medium heat and sauté the onions, carrots, celery, and potatoes. Add the chicken stock, tomatoes, oregano, basil, and bay leaf. Season with salt and pepper and bring to a boil. Reduce the heat and let simmer for about 30 to 40 minutes, partially covered.
3. Add the kidney beans, Romano beans, and spinach. Let simmer for about 5 minutes then add the asparagus and zucchini. Simmer for 3 minutes, then add the cooked pasta. Check for seasoning and serve with freshly grated Parmesan or Romano cheese.

Minestrone alla Milanese

This minestra has the addition of beef short ribs and is cooked with the bones. As the soup simmers, the fat will slowly rise to the top, at which time you can remove it.

Makes 6 servings

8 cups	chicken stock (page 123) or beef stock (page 120)	2 L
2 lb	beef short ribs, bone on, fat removed	1 kg
3	large ripe tomatoes, peeled, seeded, and diced	3
3	stalks celery, diced into ¼-inch (5 mm) pieces	3
3	large carrots, diced into ¼-inch (5 mm) pieces	3
2	medium potatoes, diced into ¼-inch (5 mm) pieces	2
1	small head escarole, shredded	1
3 cups	fresh spinach (stems removed), roughly cut	750 mL
2 cups	fresh green beans, cut into ½-inch (1 cm) pieces	500 mL
2 tsp	oregano	10 mL
¼ tsp	salt	1 mL
¼ tsp	pepper	1 mL
1½ cups	ITALPASTA Vegetable Elbows or any other small soup pasta	375 mL / 250 mL
1 cup	frozen peas, defrosted	250 mL
½ cup	Parmesan cheese, freshly grated	125 mL
3 tbsp	fresh basil, chopped	45 mL
	Parmesan cheese for sprinkling	

1. Bring the chicken or beef stock to a boil. Add the meat, tomatoes, celery, carrots, and potatoes and simmer covered for about 1 hour.
2. Add the escarole, spinach, beans, oregano, salt, and pepper and simmer for additional 15 minutes, uncovered.
3. Remove the meat with a slotted spoon. Remove the bones and gristle and cut the meat into bite-sized pieces. Return the meat to the soup and add the pasta. Bring to a boil and let simmer for 3 to 5 minutes until the pasta is *al dente*. Add the peas, stir in the Parmesan cheese and basil, and simmer for 1 or 2 more minutes. Serve with additional Parmesan cheese.

~uppa di Lenticchie

~arty soup guaranteed to warm you on a cold winter night. Make this ahead of time and when
~ated you will find flavors you never thought existed.

~es 4 to 6 servings

2 tbsp	**ITALPASTA olive oil**	**25 mL**
½ lb	**pancetta, cut into ¼-inch (5 mm) pieces**	**250 g**
1	**medium onion, diced**	**1**
2 cups	**carrots, diced into ¼-inch (5 mm) pieces**	**500 mL**
2 cups	**celery, diced into ¼-inch (5 mm) pieces**	**500 mL**
1	**ITALPASTA 28-oz (796 mL) tin plum tomatoes**	**1**
	with juice, finely diced	
6 cups	**chicken stock (page 123)**	**1.5 L**
2 tsp	**rosemary**	**10 mL**
2 tsp	**thyme**	**10 mL**
	salt and pepper to taste	
2	**19-oz (540 mL) tins lentils, drained**	**2**
3 cups	**ITALPASTA Tubetti or any small pasta**	**750 mL**
	Romano cheese, freshly grated	
	parsley, freshly chopped	

Heat the olive oil in a large soup pot and add the pancetta, onions, carrots,
and celery. Sauté over medium heat until the onions begin to brown.
Add the tomatoes, chicken stock, rosemary, thyme, salt, and pepper. Bring
to a boil and let simmer for about 20 minutes. Add the drained lentils and
continue to simmer for an additional 10 to 15 minutes.
Add the pasta and simmer until *al dente*, stirring frequently. Remove from heat
and let stand for 10 minutes. Serve garnished with Romano cheese and
parsley.

Zuppa di Orzo con Anellini

(BARLEY SOUP WITH HAM AND ANELLINI)

If you need a boost to get through the rest of the day, this soup will do it for you.

Makes 4 to 6 servings

2 tbsp	**butter**	**25 mL**
⅓ lb	**pancetta, cut into ¼-inch (5 mm) pieces**	**170 g**
1	**onion, finely diced**	**1**
3	**cloves garlic, finely minced**	**3**
2	**carrots, diced into ¼-inch (5 mm) pieces**	**2**
2	**stalks celery, diced into ¼-inch (5 mm) pieces**	**2**
1 cup	**pearl barley, soaked in water for 2 hours**	**250 mL**
6 cups	**chicken stock (page 123)**	**1.5 L**
pinch	**black pepper, freshly ground**	**pinch**
3	**bay leaves**	**3**
½ lb	**ITALPASTA Anellini**	**250 g**
½ cup	**table cream**	**125 mL**
¼ cup	**Parmesan cheese, freshly grated**	**50 mL**
2 tbsp	**parsley, freshly chopped**	**25 mL**
	salt	

1. Melt the butter in a large soup pot and add the pancetta, onions, garlic,
   carrots, and celery and sauté over medium heat until the onions and garlic
   become golden and the pancetta is crispy.
2. Add the barley, chicken stock, pepper, bay leaves, and salt to taste. Bring to a
   boil, stirring frequently. Cover, reduce the heat, and simmer for about 1 hour,
   stirring frequently.
3. Add the pasta to the soup and continue to simmer until the pasta is *al dente*,
   again stirring often. Remove bay leaves.
4. Add the cream, Parmesan cheese, and parsley. Salt to taste. Mix well and
   serve.

Basic Stocks & Sauces

With the exception of the béchamel, all these stocks and

sauces can be made in large quantities and then frozen

in serving portions. Your specialty sauces and soups will

all benefit from starting with these good basics.

Beef Stock

There is more than one way to make a flavorful beef stock or broth (used as the base for many soups, pastas, vegetable dishes, sauces, and risotto). One way is with beef bones cooked in the oven and then on the stove. The other is to buy ground beef and cook on the stove.

Makes 8 cups

METHOD USING BEEF BONES

3 lb	raw beef bones	1.5 kg
4	carrots, roughly cut	4
2	onions, peeled and quartered	2
1	celery stalk, roughly cut	1
10 cups	water	2.5 L
3	bay leaves	3
	parsley sprigs, tied	
1 cup	water or red wine (or combination)	250 mL

1. Preheat the oven to 400°F (200°C). Fill your largest roasting pan with the raw beef bones, carrots, onions, and celery. Do not pile high, rather cover the bottom of the pan evenly. Place in the oven and roast the bones and vegetables until they are well browned. Remove the pan from the oven and transfer the bones and vegetables to a large soup pot. Cover with water, add the bay leaves and tied parsley sprigs, and slowly bring to a boil.
2. In the meantime, deglaze the pan and add the juices to the pot. To do this, take the roasting pan and put it on top of one or two burners (depending on the size of the pan). Turn the heat to medium-high. Add water or red wine (or a combination of both) and, with a wooden spoon, scrape off the black, burned pieces that have stuck to the pan during roasting and mix them well with the liquid. When the entire pan has been deglazed (this is concentrated flavor and should not be discarded), pour liquid into the stockpot. When the stock has come to a boil, reduce the heat and let simmer for 2 to 3 hours. (It should never come to a rolling boil, as this will cloud the stock.) Remove bay leaves and parsley.
3. Strain through a sieve lined with cheesecloth. Allow to cool, remove the fat layer from the top then refrigerate or freeze for future use.

Makes 6 cups

METHOD USING GROUND BEEF

2 lb	lean ground beef	1 kg
2	onions, peeled and quartered	2
2	celery stalks, roughly cut	2
3	carrots, roughly cut	3
3	bay leaves	3
1	bunch of parsley sprigs	1
8 cups	water	2 L

1. Place all of the ingredients in a large stockpot. Bring this to a slow boil, skimming the surface occasionally. Cover and cook very gently for 3 to 4 hours keeping the stock just below the simmering point. Remove bay leaves and parsley.
2. Strain through a sieve lined with cheesecloth. Allow to cool, then remove the fat layer that has formed on the top. Refrigerate or freeze for future use.

Pesto

o is a sauce that has many uses. Try it on pasta or as a topping for whole broiled fish or breast of
ken. Its main use is with pasta, and many versions have been created. One of the main flavoring
edients is basil. The amount of basil used varies from recipe to recipe, depending on how fragrant the
l is and, most importantly, how strong you want the sauce to be. The following recipe should be used
as a guideline and more basil can always be added to accommodate your taste. This, of course,
ld also hold true for other ingredients such as garlic and Parmesan — although Parmesan could affect
thickness of the pesto (but this can also be countered with the use of the oil). Pesto should have a
sistency that is thicker than mayonnaise, and can then be thinned with chicken stock or other
edients such as diced, seeded tomatoes. (Note: If freezing pesto, add cheese after thawing.)

kes 2 cups

3 cups	fresh basil	750 mL
4	cloves of garlic	4
4 tbsp	pine nuts	50 mL
¾ cup	Parmesan cheese, freshly grated	175 mL
2 tbsp	pecorino cheese, freshly grated (optional)	25 mL
1 cup	ITALPASTA extra virgin olive oil	250 mL
pinch	salt	pinch
pinch	pepper	pinch

Put the basil, garlic, and pine nuts into a food processor and blend until
mixture becomes a smooth paste.
Gradually add the cheeses, using the food processor at a lower speed, until
the mixture is smooth. Slowly add the olive oil and continue to blend at a
slow speed until all the oil blends into the sauce. Add salt and pepper to
taste.

Tomato Sauce

What is an Italian kitchen without this basic sauce?

Makes 3 quarts

6	large carrots	6
4	celery stalks	4
2	medium onions	2
3	cloves of garlic	3
4 tbsp	ITALPASTA olive oil	50 mL
4	ITALPASTA 28-oz (796 mL) tins of plum tomatoes, with juice, roughly cut	4
2 tbsp	ITALPASTA tomato paste	25 mL
4 cups	water	1 L
5	sprigs of parsley	5
4	bay leaves	4
2 tsp	dried oregano	10 mL
2 tsp	rosemary	10 mL
2 tsp	thyme	10 mL
pinch	salt	pinch
pinch	pepper	pinch

1. Using a meat grinder or food processor, mince the carrots, celery, onions, and
   garlic so they come out as fine as possible. (This is so the vegetables don't
   show in the sauce.)
2. In a large soup or sauce pot, heat the olive oil and sauté the vegetables until
   the onions begin to change color. Add the tomatoes, tomato paste, and the
   rest of the ingredients. Stir well with a whisk and bring to a boil. Reduce the
   heat and let simmer for 1½ to 2 hours. The sauce should begin to thicken.
   Skim the oil that rises to the top as the sauce is simmering. Remove the bay
   leaves and the parsley, let cool, and refrigerate, freeze, or use right away.

Salsa alla Bolognese

(TOMATO MEAT SAUCE)

Your lasagna will only be as good as your sauce. Add more ground beef or veal if you like a meatier taste.

Makes 3 quarts

5	large carrots	5
4	celery stalks	4
2	large onions	2
4	cloves garlic	4
3 tbsp	ITALPASTA olive oil	45 mL
2 lb	lean ground beef	1 kg
2 tsp	oregano	10 mL
2 tsp	thyme	10 mL
2 tsp	rosemary	10 mL
pinch	salt	pinch
	pepper to taste	
12 cups	ITALPASTA canned plum tomatoes, with juice, roughly cut	3 L
4 tbsp	ITALPASTA tomato paste	50 mL
3 tbsp	sugar (optional)	45 mL
3 cups	water	750 mL
3	bay leaves	3
5	parsley sprigs tied together	5

1. Using a meat grinder or food processor, grind the carrots, celery, onions, and garlic.
2. In a large soup or stockpot, heat the oil and sauté the ground vegetables until the onions turn golden.
3. Add the beef, oregano, thyme, rosemary, salt, and pepper. Continue to sauté, stirring with a wooden spoon until the ground beef is cooked.
4. Add the tomatoes, tomato paste, sugar, water, bay leaves, and parsley. Stir well and bring to a boil. Reduce the heat and, partially covered, let simmer for about 2 hours, stirring often and skimming the fat with a ladle as it rises to the top. When the sauce has thickened, remove the bay leaves and parsley. Check for seasoning and let cool, or use as needed.

Béchamel

(WHITE SAUCE)

This is a basic sauce used in both French and Italian cooking, and can be used hot or cold as an ingredient in many sauces and dishes. To remove lumps, strain the sauce through a fine sieve. The sau[ce] is kept fairly bland as it will be flavored when used in a recipe.

Makes 5 cups

2 tbsp	unsalted butter	25 mL
1 cup	all-purpose flour	250 mL
4 cups	milk, divided	1 L
½ tsp	nutmeg	2 mL
pinch	salt	pinch
pinch	white pepper	pinch

1. Melt the butter in a medium-sized saucepan.
2. Over medium-low heat, stir in the flour with a whisk and continue to cook for 3 to 4 minutes, stirring constantly. When the flour mixture (roux) looks like it is beginning to change color, add half the milk, increase the heat and whisk until smooth.
3. Add the remaining milk, the nutmeg, and the salt and pepper and whisk un[til] smooth. Lower the heat and simmer for 3 to 5 minutes.

Chicken Stock

re are a number of ways to make a good and flavorful chicken stock. One way is to freeze chicken
turkey bones as you use the meat. Remember to skim the fat as you cook the stock. The stock should
be seasoned other than with bay leaves and whole bunches of parsley. It can be used in a variety
shes and will be seasoned accordingly.

es 7 cups

METHOD 1

3 lb	chicken and turkey bones	1.5 kg
3	bay leaves	3
2	bunches of parsley, tied together	2
4	carrots, chopped	4
1	celery stalk, chopped	1
2	onions, cut into ¼-inch (5 mm) pieces	2

Cover the bones well in water, remembering that you are going to let the stock
simmer for about 2 hours and reduce by at least one quarter. Add bay leaves,
tied parsley bunches, carrots, celery, and onion pieces and bring to a boil.
Reduce the heat and let the stock simmer for 1 to 2 hours. Remove bay leaves
and parsley. If you wish, you can skim the fat off the top as it rises.

METHOD 2

Use a whole chicken and the same ingredients as in Method 1.
After simmering for 2 hours, remove the chicken, bay leaves, and parsley.
When the stock has cooled, strain and then refrigerate. The fat will rise to the
top and solidify and can be removed without losing any of the stock.

Fish Stock

This is a stock that is best made with fish heads that can be purchased at your local fish market. As with
other stocks, spicing is not recommended, as these will be added when the stock is used in a recipe. This
stock can be used for many seafood dishes and a base for soups. If you are making it with a particular
dish in mind — one that requires certain spices and herbs — these can be used in moderation.

Makes 8 cups

4 lb	fish heads, bones, or tails (or a combination of all three), enough to fill three-quarters of a large pot	2 kg
4	large carrots, cut into chunks	4
3	celery stalks, cut into chunks	3
2	onions, quartered	2
2	cloves garlic	2
3	bay leaves	3
1	small bunch of parsley	1

1. Put all ingredients into a large pot and cover with cold water. Bring to a slow
   boil and, with the lid partially covering the pot, reduce the heat and let
   simmer for about 1 to 1½ hours. (Do not stir as this might cloud the stock.)
2. Remove bay leaves and parsley. Pour through a strainer lined with cheesecloth
   and let cool. Refrigerate or freeze for further use.

CHAPTER NINE

Pasta Salads

Pasta salads are good examples of all that is fine about

Italian cooking. The colors of vegetables are at their most

vivid. The herbs are fresh. The meats and seafood are

tender. The oil is fruity and the dressings simple and

clean. In a pasta salad, the colors and flavors of all the

ingredients combine and shine.

nsalata di Conchiglie alla Mascarpone

(ASTA SALAD WITH MASCARPONE DRESSING)

…carpone is a cheese found in many regions of Italy. It has traditionally been made from fresh cream …has been used as a dessert cheese served with sugar and fruit. Here, it makes a wonderful creamy …ssing for pasta, vegetables, and fruits.

…kes 4 to 6 servings

½ lb	**ITALPASTA Shells (Small Conchiglie)**	250 g
1 tbsp	**ITALPASTA extra virgin olive oil**	15 mL
1 cup	**black olives, pitted and sliced**	250 mL
4	**green onions, sliced into ½-inch (1 cm) pieces**	4
1	**red pepper, julienne***	1
1	**yellow pepper, julienne**	1
pinch	**salt**	pinch
pinch	**pepper**	pinch

…essing

1 tbsp	**ITALPASTA balsamic vinegar**	15 mL
⅓ cup	**ITALPASTA extra virgin olive oil**	75 mL
½ cup	**mascarpone, thinned with a little milk**	125 mL
2 tbsp	**sugar**	25 mL

*Julienne is strips 2 inches (5 cm) long by ¼ inch (5 mm) wide

Bring a large pot of lightly salted water to a boil and cook the pasta *al dente*. Rinse in cold water and drain.

In a large mixing bowl, mix the cooked pasta with 1 tbsp (15 mL) of the olive oil, black olives, green onions, peppers, salt, and pepper.

Dressing: In a small mixing bowl, mix the balsamic vinegar and ⅓ cup (75 mL) of olive oil and beat in the mascarpone.

Toss or stir the pasta and vegetables with the dressing and serve at room temperature.

Insalata di Fusilli e Penne

(PASTA SALAD WITH ROASTED VEGETABLES)

You might say that this salad has everything in it but the kitchen sink. Myriad colors, textures, and tastes make this dish a great lunch or part of a buffet. Multi-colored pasta is a nice touch in this colorful dish.

Makes 4 to 6 servings

½ lb	**ITALPASTA Vegetable Fusilli**	250 g
½ lb	**ITALPASTA Penne**	250 g
3	**red bell peppers**	3
1	**medium eggplant**	1
1 cup	**artichoke hearts, quartered**	250 mL
10	**green olives, pitted and sliced**	10
10	**black olives, pitted and sliced**	10
2 tbsp	**capers**	25 mL
1	**avocado, peeled and cut into ½-inch (1 cm) chunks**	1
1 cup	**ITALPASTA extra virgin olive oil**	250 mL
1 tbsp	**ITALPASTA balsamic vinegar**	15 mL
2 tbsp	**fresh basil, chopped**	25 mL
2 tbsp	**fresh parsley, chopped**	25 mL
1 tbsp	**lemon juice**	15 mL
¼ cup	**Parmesan cheese, freshly grated**	50 mL
¼ cup	**Romano cheese, freshly grated**	50 mL
pinch	**salt**	pinch
pinch	**black pepper, freshly ground**	pinch

1. Bring a large pot of lightly salted water to a boil and cook the fusilli and penne *al dente*, rinse in cold water, and drain well.
2. Roast the red peppers under the broiler or over an open flame until the skin is charred on all sides. Place in a covered bowl for about 15 minutes.
3. Roast the eggplant the same way as the peppers and allow to cool in a bowl, uncovered.
4. Remove the red peppers from the bowl, cut them in half, remove the core and scrape away the skin and seeds. Cut into ½-inch (1 cm) squares.
5. Remove the eggplant from the bowl, cut the top off, and peel away the skin. Cut lengthwise, remove the seeds, and cut into ½-inch (1 cm) squares.
6. In a mixing bowl, add the pasta, peppers, eggplant, and the rest of the ingredients one at a time, saving the Parmesan and Romano cheeses until last. Add salt and black pepper if desired. Toss or stir well, and serve at room temperature.

Insalata di Ditali con Fave
(SALAD WITH DITALI PASTA AND FAVA BEANS)

pasta and fava bean salad: colorful, healthy, and a wonderful lunch. This salad should always be served
room temperature rather than directly from the refrigerator. They can be served as a main course or side
h to almost any meal.

akes 4 to 6 servings

1 lb	**ITALPASTA Ditali**	**500 g**
1½ lb	**fava beans**	**750 g**
3 cups	**chicken stock (page 123)**	**750 mL**
1 cup	**water**	**250 mL**
3	**plum tomatoes, seeded and diced**	**3**
7	**strips of lean bacon, fried or baked and very finely chopped**	**7**

ressing

2	**egg yolks**	**2**
½ cup	**ITALPASTA olive oil**	**125 mL**
¼ cup	**ITALPASTA balsamic vinegar (a little more or less as, you like it)**	**50 mL**
1 tbsp	**lemon juice**	**15 mL**
¼ cup	**Parmesan cheese, freshly grated**	**50 mL**
¼ cup	**Romano cheese, freshly grated**	**50 mL**
½ tsp	**white pepper**	**2 mL**
¼ cup	**reserved fava bean liquid**	**50 mL**

Bring a large pot of lightly salted water to a boil and cook the pasta *al dente*.
Rinse in cold water and drain.

In a large pot, soak the fava beans for 12 hours in lukewarm water then add
the beans, chicken stock, and water. Bring to a boil and let simmer for about
1 hour or until the beans are tender but firm. Add more water if necessary.
Drain the beans and refresh in cold water. Reserve the cooking liquid.

Dressing: In a stainless steel whipping bowl, add the egg yolks and gently
whisk in the oil, balsamic vinegar, lemon juice, Parmesan cheese, Romano
cheese, white pepper, and the reserved broth from the fava beans.

In another mixing bowl, combine the diced tomatoes, cooked ditali, fava
beans, and bacon bits. Gently mix the ingredients well, adding the dressing at
the same time. Sprinkle with a mixture of Romano and Parmesan cheese and
serve.

Insalata alla Niçoise
(RADIATOR PASTA SALAD)

There is a tuna salad; then there is my version. A little different, and a lot better. Serve this as all salads
should be served: at room temperature.

Makes 6 servings

½ lb	**ITALPASTA Vegetable Radiators**	**250 g**
3 cups	**broccoli florets**	**750 mL**
1 cup	**French cut green beans, cut in half diagonally**	**250 mL**
½ cup	**black olives, pitted and sliced**	**125 mL**
6	**scallions, sliced with the green tops**	**6**
1 cup	**pine nuts (slivered almonds, walnuts, or a combination of all)**	**250 mL**
1	**6½-oz (184 g) tin solid white tuna, drained**	**1**
1 cup	**cherry tomatoes, halved**	**250 mL**
12	**basil leaves, finely chopped**	**12**

Dressing

⅓ cup	**ITALPASTA extra virgin olive oil**	**75 mL**
3 tbsp	**ITALPASTA balsamic vinegar**	**45 mL**
2 tbsp	**lemon juice**	**25 mL**
4 tbsp	**poppy seeds**	**50 mL**

1. Bring a pot of lightly salted water to a boil and cook the pasta *al dente*. Drain
   and allow to cool by spreading onto a baking dish and drizzling with olive oil.
2. Bring another pot of water to a boil and cook the broccoli and beans together
   for about 1 minute or until they are cooked but still crispy (longer if you like
   them softer). Rinse in cold water and drain.
3. Mix the vegetables with the olives, scallions, pine nuts, tuna, tomatoes, basil,
   and pasta. Add olive oil, balsamic vinegar, and lemon juice. Serve sprinkled
   with poppy seeds.

Fusilli con Caponata

(TOMATO FUSILLI AND EGGPLANT SALAD)

You need to plan ahead for this salad, but if you love eggplant, it's worth it. When you want to serve it, you need only cook the pasta, allow it to cool, mix with the eggplant, and serve. This is an excellent luncheon entrée or a side dish for almost any dinnertime meal.

Makes 6 to 8 servings

1 lb	ITALPASTA Fusilli	500 g
2	medium-large eggplants (about 3 pounds/1.5 kg)	2
pinch	course salt	pinch
1 cup	ITALPASTA extra virgin olive oil	250 mL
1	large onion, cut into ¼-inch (5 mm) slices	1
6	ribs celery, cut into ½-inch (1 cm) lengths, blanched for 1 minute	6
1 cup	Sicilian green olives, pitted and sliced	250 mL
½ cup	capers	125 mL
1 cup	fresh plum tomatoes, peeled, seeded, and diced	250 mL
3 tbsp	ITALPASTA tomato paste	45 mL
½ cup	red wine vinegar	125 mL
3 tbsp	sugar	45 mL
3 tbsp	dark raisins	45 mL
2 tbsp	fresh rosemary	25 mL
3 tbsp	fresh thyme	45 mL
pinch	salt	pinch
pinch	pepper	pinch
½ cup	slivered almonds, toasted (or pine nuts)	125 mL

1. Peel the eggplants and cut into ¾-inch (2 cm) cubes. Sprinkle with coarse salt and drain in a colander weighted down, for one hour.
2. Sauté the onion in ½ cup (250 mL) of the olive oil for about 1 minute (do not brown). Add the blanched celery and cook a minute longer. Add the olives, capers, tomatoes, tomato paste, vinegar, sugar, and raisins and set aside.
3. Rinse the eggplants well and dry in a kitchen towel.
4. Heat the remainder of the olive oil in a large skillet and fry the eggplant in batches until golden on all sides, adding more oil if necessary. Drain on paper towels.
5. Add the eggplant to the sauce with the rosemary and thyme, and simmer for another 10 minutes. Season with salt and pepper. Cool and refrigerate for 24 hours.
6. To serve the salad, bring a large pot of lightly salted water to a boil and cook the pasta *al dente*. Drain well and spread onto a large cookie sheet to cool. Mix the pasta with the eggplant mixture, check for seasoning, and serve sprinkled with the toasted slivered almonds. Serve chilled or at room temperature.

Insalata di Fettuccine con Asparagi e Salmone

(FETTUCCINE WITH ASPARAGUS AND SMOKED SALMON SALAD)

Smoked salmon should always be served at room temperature rather than hot. If you love smoked salmon, fresh asparagus, and fresh herbs, than you will love this salad. A great appetizer or lunch.

Makes 4 to 6 servings as a luncheon entrée, or 8 to 10 servings as a side dish or appetizer

1 lb	ITALPASTA Fettuccine	500 g
1 lb	fresh asparagus, cleaned, trimmed, and cut into 1-inch (2.5 cm) pieces	500 g
6 oz	smoked salmon, cut into strips	175 g
2 tbsp	fresh dill, chopped	25 mL
3 tbsp	fresh parsley, chopped	45 mL
3 tbsp	fresh chives, chopped	45 mL
2 tbsp	fresh basil, chopped	25 mL
2 tbsp	capers	25 mL
1 tbsp	lemon juice	15 mL
3 tbsp	ITALPASTA extra virgin olive oil	45 mL
pinch	salt	pinch
pinch	pepper	pinch
¼ cup	Parmesan cheese, freshly grated	50 mL

1. Bring a large pot of lightly salted water to a boil and cook the pasta *al dente*. Rinse in cold water and drain.
2. Bring another pot of lightly salted water to a boil and cook or steam the asparagus so that it is still crunchy. Rinse in cold water and drain.
3. In a large mixing bowl, add the fettuccine, asparagus, salmon slices, herbs, capers, lemon juice (more if desired), olive oil, salt, and pepper. Mix well and serve.

Insalata di Pasta alla Genovese

(PASTA SALAD WITH ROASTED RED PEPPERS, ONIONS, AND GENOA SALAMI)

This salad makes a great lunch or a buffet salad, best served at room temperature. Fresh, sliced sweet red peppers can be used instead of the roasted red peppers if time is short.

Makes 4 to 6 servings

½ lb	ITALPASTA Radiators	250 g
6 tbsp	ITALPASTA extra virgin olive oil	90 mL
3	large red bell peppers	3
½ lb	Genoa salami, julienne*	250 g
1	large red onion, julienne	1
4	cloves garlic, finely chopped	4
2 tsp	Spanish paprika	10 mL
2	large tomatoes, seeded and diced	2
pinch	salt	pinch
pinch	black pepper, freshly ground	pinch
¾ cup	sour cream	175 mL
3	dashes of tabasco sauce (or ½ tsp (2 mL) of crushed chili peppers)	3
¼ cup	Romano cheese, freshly grated	50 mL

*Julienne is strips 2 inches (5 cm) long by ¼ inch (5 mm) wide

1. Bring a large pot of lightly salted water to a boil. Add the pasta and cook *al dente*. Drain and transfer to a large mixing bowl. Sprinkle with olive oil and let cool at room temperature.
2. Roast the red peppers under a broiler or over an open flame until the skin is charred on all sides. Transfer them to a paper bag or covered bowl and let sit for about 20 minutes. Cut them in half, remove the core, and scrape away the skin. Cut into strips.
3. Heat 2 tbsp (25 mL) of the oil in a large skillet and sauté the onions until golden. Add the strips of salami to the onions and sauté for another minute, tossing or stirring frequently. Reduce the heat slightly, add the garlic, and continue to sauté for another minute or so. Add the paprika and stir well. Add the red peppers, tomatoes, salt, and pepper and cook for an additional 1 to 2 minutes, then remove from the heat.
4. Transfer to a mixing bowl and allow to cool slightly. Add the sour cream, tabasco sauce, and remaining olive oil and mix well. Add the pasta and the Romano cheese, toss well, let sit at room temperature for a least 30 minutes and serve. (Do not put in the fridge to cool.)

Insalata di Penne e Capocollo

(PENNE SALAD WITH CAPOCOLLO)

I love capocollo ham just about as much as I love fresh seafood. My preference is the spicy one. Instead of a capocollo sandwich (which I love), try this salad, you'll love it too. Serve at room temperature as a luncheon entrée or a side dish for supper.

Makes 4 to 6 servings

½ lb	ITALPASTA Penne	250 g
⅓ cup	ITALPASTA extra virgin olive oil	75 mL
2 tbsp	red wine vinegar or lemon juice	25 mL
6	anchovy fillets, finely chopped	6
6 oz	capocollo ham (sweet or spicy), julienne*	175 g
1 cup	black olives, pitted and sliced	250 mL
4	green onions, sliced	4
¼ cup	Romano cheese, freshly grated	50 mL
¼ cup	Parmesan cheese, freshly grated	50 mL
pinch	salt	pinch
pinch	pepper	pinch

*Julienne is strips 2 inches (5 cm) long by ¼ inch (5 mm) wide

1. Bring a large pot of slightly salted water to a boil. Cook the penne *al dente*, rinse in cold water, and drain.
2. In a large mixing bowl, add all the ingredients and mix or toss well. Check for seasoning and use additional vinegar or lemon juice if necessary.

Insalata di Pasta con Prosciutto e Piselli

(PASTA SALAD WITH PROSCIUTTO AND PEAS)

Salads are thought of as first or second courses to a meal, or eaten with the meal. I have always felt that a first course should prepare the mouth for what is to come. This salad will do just that.

Makes 4 to 6 servings

Anchovy Mixture

5	**ITALPASTA anchovies**	5
2	**cloves garlic**	2
½ tsp	**black pepper, freshly ground**	2 mL
2 tbsp	**ITALPASTA olive oil**	25 mL
⅓ cup	**Parmesan cheese, freshly grated**	75 mL

Dressing

⅓ cup	**ITALPASTA extra virgin olive oil**	75 mL
2 tbsp	**red wine vinegar**	25 mL
2 tbsp	**lemon juice**	25 mL
1 tsp	**dried thyme**	5 mL
1 tsp	**dry mustard**	5 mL
2	**dashes of Tabasco sauce**	2
2	**dashes of Worcestershire sauce**	2
1	**egg**	1

Salad

1 tbsp	**ITALPASTA olive oil**	15 mL
1 lb	**ITALPASTA Shells or Tubetti**	500 g
2 cups	**peas, fresh or frozen**	500 mL
1	**large red onion, julienne**	1
½ lb	**prosciutto ham, thinly sliced, julienne**	250 g

*Julienne is strips 2 inches (5 cm) long by ¼ inch (5 mm) wide

1. Combine the anchovies, garlic, black pepper, and olive oil in a blender and purée until smooth. Add the grated cheese and continue to purée until combined.
2. Place the olive oil, red wine vinegar, lemon juice, mustard, tabasco, and Worcestershire sauce in a mixing bowl and add the anchovy mixture. Add the raw egg to the mixture and whisk until well combined.
3. Heat the oil in a skillet and sauté the onions with the thyme until the onions are a rich golden color. Transfer the onions to a large mixing bowl and allow to cool at room temperature.
4. Meanwhile, bring a large pot of lightly salted water to a boil and cook the pasta *al dente*. Drain in a large colander, sprinkle with olive oil, and transfer to another bowl to cool, again at room temperature.
5. Cook the peas, rinse in cold water, and drain.
6. Add the peas to the onions, prosciutto, and the dressing and mix well. Add the pasta, toss or stir well, and serve at room temperature.

Glossary of Ingredients

Your soups, salads, risottos, and other creations are only as good as what you put into them. The following tips on buying, storing, and cooking with some of the most common ingredients in Italian cooking will help you achieve the best possible results.

Anchovy Fillets: A staple item in the kitchen pantry of any Italian cook. When used with discretion, they can add a distinct flavor to many sauces. Anchovies may also be used in stuffings for baked vegetables, or mashed in oil-based sauces for boiled vegetables. Do not overcook, or the anchovies will become bitter and unpleasant.

Artichokes: When buying fresh, don't choose specimens that are hairy — the heart will be tough and tasteless. Look for leaves that are pressed tightly against each other. Open leaves are a sign that the artichoke is overripe.

Basil: One of the most popular and widely used Italian herbs, basil is also one of the most delicate. Once cut from the plant, it does not hold up very long. Fresh basil will last two to three days in the refrigerator if wrapped in damp paper towels and placed in a plastic bag. If you wish to keep it longer, basil may be preserved in olive oil or between layers of coarse salt in a tightly sealed jar. (It will lose some of its color, but will retain most of its flavor). Do not used dried basil as a substitute for fresh — the flavors bear no resemblance to one another.

Butter: Despite the widespread use of olive oil, butter is equally important in the Italian kitchen. Use only unsalted — or sweet — butter; its flavor is more delicate. Take care when storing, though. Sweet butter is more perishable than the salted variety, and it readily absorbs the flavors of nearby food. Keep covered, and always store in the refrigerator.

Capers: Capers are the small, unopened buds of a bush that grow wild in Mediterranean countries. They are used frequently in Sicilian cooking and may be added to sauces for pastas, meat, fish or stuffings. Capers are usually packed in brine and should be drained before using, unless otherwise specified.

Carrots: Resist the urge to buy the largest you can find — the cor will be tough, and the taste bitter.

Garlic: When choosing garlic, select heads that are firm to the touch. Garlic should be chopped finely, rather than squeezed through a press. (The latter method tends to release only the juice leaving most of the pulp behind). Never substitute garlic powder garlic salt for fresh garlic. Do not overcook garlic or it will burn. I this happens, the only alternative is to start again.

Gorgonzola: This is a blue-veined cheese made with cow's milk. usually ripens in two to three months. Young gorgonzolas are mil creamy, and sweet. Aged varieties are spicy and strong. The blue veins are produced by inserting long copper, steel, or brass needle into the cheese, allowing air to enter and form a mold. The more holes, the tangier the cheese. Gorgonzola is best if eaten within a day or two of purchase.

Herbs: In general, it's best to use fresh herbs whenever possible. They add a more delicate flavor to the dish being prepared. The exceptions to this rule are oregano and rosemary, which retain most of their flavor when dried. Use all herbs with restraint. Seasonings should complement the main ingredients, not overpower them.

Mascarpone: A creamy cheese made from cow's milk. It is best known as an ingredient in tiramisu, but can also be added to sauces to create a creamier consistency.

Mozzarella: True mozzarella is made from water buffalo milk — and is not easily found in North America. It is generally stored in water, and should be used within a day or two of purchase. Fresh mozzarella is often paired with sliced tomatoes or roasted peppers and served as a first course.

Mushrooms: When buying mushrooms, avoid those that are bruised or discolored. To store, wrap in a slightly damp paper towel and keep in the refrigerator. Never wrap mushrooms in plastic — the trapped moisture will create mold. Washing mushrooms can alter their texture. To clean, use a soft brush to remove any dirt. If dirt remains, pass quickly under a stream of cold water, taking care not to wet the undersides.

Olive oil: Always use the best extra virgin olive oil you can afford. Olive oils have a shelf life of approximately one year. Store in a cool, dark place — never in the refrigerator and never near a source of heat. Do not add the remnants of an old bottle of oil to a new bottle. The older oil will have a stronger flavor that will permeate the new.

Tomatoes: Remember that different types of tomatoes are suited for different purposes. Plum tomatoes, for example, have few seeds, are small and fleshy, and carry less water than other varieties — perfect for making sauces. Beefsteak tomatoes, while tasty when ripe, are too watery for sauces. Cherry tomatoes are often sweet and nicely colored, making them ideal for almost any use, but peeling and seeding takes patience. Store tomatoes at room temperature — refrigeration will change the flavor. If good, fresh tomatoes are not available, choose high-quality canned tomatoes in their own juices.

Vegetables: Ideally, it's best to use vegetables that are in season, and bought straight from the farm. Since that's not always possible, follow these guidelines when buying from your local supermarket or green grocer. Avoid vegetables that are bruised, discolored, spotty, wrinkled, or wilted. When choosing leafy vegetables, look for nice color — there should be no yellow leaves, and no discoloration at leaf edges. Use all vegetables quickly. The longer they are stored, the more flavor they lose.

Acknowledgments

This book was made possible by a team of very talented and dedicated people. They all deserve special thanks and acknowledgment for their participation.

Here are a few, however, who deserve special mention:

Terry Kohl, whose phenomenal knowledge and culinary expertise made this book a reality.

Ed Della Vedova, our wonderful creative director.

Philip Dean, whose stunning photography graces these pages.

Bruce MacDonald at Big Brothers. It was a great privilege to work with Big Brothers and Sisters of Canada. It has given us an opportunity to help a very worthy cause. We would like to thank everyone at Big Brothers and Sisters of Canada connected with this project.

Index